PRAISE FOR CRO..... ... . LUIRE

"Heidi Fuller-love has written a welcome antidote to all those jolly Frenchman books by Peter Mayle. This is a modern horror story about moving home, packed with wicked humour, sticky camembert and plumbing tales to make your hair stand on end. Definitely what I always secretly imagined was the true story behind all those jolly 'moving to France' tales." Tim (Pig) Storer, Pie manufacturer, Leicester.

"Well I'm French and I certainly recognise myself in this book – I suppose you could say that's the best praise anyone could ask for?" Marie Lamouroux, French housewife.

"Ms Fuller-love has taken French toilet humour to hitherto unconsidered heights." John Dunn, undertaker, Cornwall.

"Suffocatingly funny." Janet Astles, artist, Scunthorpe.

This book is dedicated to Arnolda Albertha Oosterholt, who knew all about leaving home.

CROSSING THE LOIRE

Heidi Fuller-love

FPP *France Pronde Publications*

Printed in Victoria, Canada

Note for Librarians: a cataloguing record for this book that includes Dewey Classification and US Library of Congress numbers is available from the National Library of Canada. The complete cataloguing record can be obtained from the National Library's online database at:
www.nlc-bnc.ca/amicus/index-e.html
ISBN 1-4120-2425-0

TRAFFORD

This book was published on-demand in cooperation with Trafford Publishing.
On-demand publishing is a unique process and service of making a book available for retail sale to the public taking advantage of on-demand manufacturing and Internet marketing. On-demand publishing includes promotions, retail sales, manufacturing, order fulfilment, accounting and collecting royalties on behalf of the author.

Suite 6E, 2333 Government St., Victoria, B.C. V8T 4P4, CANADA
Phone 250-383-6864   Toll-free 1-888-232-4444 (Canada & US)
Fax 250-383-6804   E-mail sales@trafford.com   Web site www.trafford.com
TRAFFORD PUBLISHING IS A DIVISION OF TRAFFORD HOLDINGS LTD.
Trafford Catalogue #04-0253   www.trafford.com/robots/04-0253.html

10   9   8   7   6   5   4   3   2   1

CONTENTS

CROSSING THE LOIRE

We weren't just crossing a river. We were crossing over into a whole new way of life..

CHAPTER ONE

Punching at the lumbering 'Deux Chevaux', buffeting its badly reefed canvas roof, the banshee wind snatches at its glass ears, flaps them open, curses, bangs them shut again.

"*Non, rien de rien. Non, je ne regrette rien,*" sobs Edith Piaf over our crackling car radio. It is the perfect - if melodramatic - accompaniment to my mental farewell. We'd left our old life behind us, shed the town and its habits like a snake sheds its skin, and were heading for a distant point splashed with jam on the map. Mouzon. Forty, or so, inhabitants and twice as many cows. Somewhere in the heart of France.

When I first told my friends that I was planning to leave my cosy flat in downtown Greenwich, and head out to live in the wilds of another country with a Frenchman I met on holiday, they stared at me as if I was doomed.

"Doomed!" said eyes that would no longer look into mine. "Doomed!" whispered lips which snickered behind my back.

And even when I got out my much pored-over map and showed them the village of Mouzon, nestling between a large marmalade stain, a glob of camembert and the vine-grower's district of Bordeaux, they didn't seem particularly convinced. After all I already had everything a *gal* could ask for: posh flat, good job, great mates (!!), what the heck did I mean when I said I wanted 'more?'

To tell the truth I'd already asked myself most of the questions they were firing at me, at least a hundred times. In guise of reply I could only mangle a bit of Montaigne and stutter something about knowing what I was r-r-running from - joggers with elbows like meat cleavers, the horrors of road rage and that cleverly disguised indifference called "politically correct" - but not being exactly sure what it was I was r-r-running to.

To cover my confusion I sneaked off to the local library and there, amongst a host of frivolous tomes which seemed to be exhorting me to fly away and have fun in Caracas, or strip to a string and get flustered in Copacabaña, I found a dusty relic, that was surely once a book, entitled, *'La Vie et les Temps de la Charente.'*

Ignoring the lumpy title I had a peek inside and was instantly.. horrified. I must admit that before moving there I'd never heard of the area know as *'La Charente'* before. I was perfectly *'au fait'* with Cognac, of course, although I had this vague vision of the town being like some mini-Monaco: totally independent from the rest of the world and having its own rules and regulations and currency stamped with the head of some notorious Brandy Baron, but I had no idea that the city, which is soaked in the ethers of France's most famous booze, was actually one of the main towns of the region where I was planning to take up residence.

Shedding instant light on my pig ignorance, then, I read: *"La Charente* is the poorer sister to neighbouring Dordogne. Its main exports are *'Pineau'*, a sweet, fortified wine, the world-renowned spirit called Cognac, and slippers, known as *'Charentaises',* which are exported as far afield as Thailand."

Slippers to Thailand? The notion of anyone exporting slippers to Thailand really made my mind boggle.

"The Charente people are known for their slow pace of life, and Mediterranean ways, hence their nickname, *'cagouille',* which is patois for 'snail'."

I chuckled at the vision of a snail in slippers, sporting a beret, and carrying a crisp brown baguette.

3

"The 'Charentais' people nurse a historic hatred of the English, who spent a great deal of time here during the 100 years war," the book continued. At this point I put it back to mouldering on its shelf and decided I'd wait and see for myself.

"Sure you won't be homesick?" my flat mate asked. She was hovering out on the landing, torn between the horrified fascination of watching me pack, and the guilty excitation of listening out for the kettle's shrill whistle which was the signal she could legitimately clock-off for another of those comforting cuppas which bribed her through her - writing - day.

"Homesick?" I remember thinking as I stared around me at the dismal Greenwich council flat we'd shared for so many years. It struck me that I'd been here so long the bedroom carpet was worn to a thread by my passing..

'Homesick?' A goods train rattled past, and its screech below neatly synchronised with the kettle's whistle above. I gazed out through the fast-dimming window at the drizzle-and-smog soaked fug of another waning city day and just shook my head. How could I tell her that I was far more sick of home, than I was ever likely to be homesick?

A few days later, when I'd crossed the Channel with all my worldly goods in tow and stood-by whilst Fabrice informed his family that he intended to leave his modern apartment, with all mod-cons, in the heart of chic Versailles and set up house in an ancestral family hovel in the depths of the Charente countryside, I met with the same - brutal - incomprehension.

Maybe it was normal for me to do this sort of thing, because I was 'an English' and everyone knew that the English were hopelessly eccentric, but Fabrice was young, well-educated and French, and young, well-educated Frenchmen do not just 'up sticks' and head off to start a new life in the countryside. It just isn't done.

Usually at each others throats for reasons ranging from the size of wreaths bought each year to put on the family's various ancestral tombs at '*Le Toussaint*', to who would inherit what when grandma died, Fabrice's family were united for once, then, in their condemnation of 'our foolhardy departure'.

One misty morning in late October, they assembled on the pavement to wave us off: mother, sister, half-brother, and even la petite grandmamma, all wearing that smug air of disgust, mingled with told-you-so glee and just a *soupçon* of downright contempt, which is generally reserved for greenhorns setting out, unarmed, to meet the head-hunters of Borneo.

5

"You'll be back!" Fabrice's mother cackled from the safety of her Versailles sidewalk. "They're all peasants out there, you'll see. Just a bunch of local yokels!"

The car juddered forward. Pots and pans rattled. The cat peed on the backseat.

"But we're only moving to the countryside," I protested feebly.

Her shriek echoed after us down the elegant, shop-lined street. "Only?" I heard her cry. "What do you mean, 'only'?"

France is twice the size of the United Kingdom and at least 50 percent of the population live in towns, which leaves an awful lot of space in between. Coming from a country where land is sold by centimetres, and property is not so much a dwelling space as a major financial investment, I found it hard to make sense of the vast, unbuilt-upon expanses we travelled through after leaving Versailles. How could there be so many abandoned houses? Who would be crazy enough to discard so many of their vital assets to poison ivy? Already the rules which had, hitherto, regulated my existence were starting not to make sense. I was beginning to understand that what I'd taken to be 'the norm', was just a matter of perspective - that you only have to change certain criteria to change everything.

With a howling gale from gaping holes in the side doors gusting our hair out behind us in romantic disarray, we wallowed, in our clapped-out old banger, down the arrow-straight main road towards Chartres. On either side of us the fields were ploughed to rough chocolate and seemed to drag everything down into their heavy, horizontal lines. Only the cathedral stood on the horizon like a miracle, defying the local laws of gravity.

If it was difficult coping with the notion of so many ruins, it wasn't easy getting used to Fabrice's *'Deux Chevaux'* either. The suspension on a 'duck' is unlike any other car's. Riding in it for long distances is like spending the day out in a mobile trampoline and we got hoarse from shouting out hump-backed bridges in advance, and backache from hunching over like a brace of crazed Quasimodos at the sight of potholes in order to avoid thumping our heads on the canvas roof. On one particularly 'gruyèred' stretch of road we narrowly avoided a major pile-up. The sight of the two of us bobbing up and down like mating sparrows was too much for fellow motorists, who craned around to stare after us, instead of at the road, and veered into the path of oncoming cars.

After Chartres the sky turned pink, rammed the sun, like a soft-boiled egg, deep into it's back pocket and curdled slowly black. In the dimming light everything seemed vaguely menacing. On a tree-lined road stolen from Monet we were assailed by a jumble of shopping malls. A cardboard tongue above a slipper factory jeered at us, ovoid characters clutching wine glasses above the plastic-pillared portal of a wine shop leered at us, and in the gathering dusk chunky hams in muslin nighties, loops of chorizo and a pale pink pig's cadaver strung up in a butchers shop seemed like ex-voto designed to conjure some particularly gory evil-eye. Everything seemed strange, unknown, threatening and I found myself thinking of Mouzon. In my mind's eye I saw the one main street, a tiny rash of houses, the herds of cows - and all that fresh air where I'd been used to fresh concrete! I groaned inwardly. "What on earth was I doing?"

To take my mind off things Fabrice told me about my new home. He started with what, for him, was the most important feature: the toilet facilities.

"My father was in the army. He fought in Indochina and everything, you know, but he always claimed his worst mission was cleaning out the black hole at the bottom of our garden. The problem for us was that he was often sent abroad. If we were lucky he wangled leave every few weeks, which meant the black hole was emptied. If not," he broke off and shuddered expressively.

8

"Sometimes father was away as long as six months. Can you imagine? At such delicate times my mother arranged the routine of our daily doings with a military precision that would have made father proud. To aid us in our deadly battle against bacteria, she created a sort-of armour for us, made out of shirts, coats, gloves, whatever she could lay her hands on. Even in the height of summer she would shield us like this and then march us, one by one, down to the dreaded hole. Unfortunately, rolled up in our cocoons like five, un-hatched, butterflies the actual operation was just about impossible. One after another, the five of us were forced to hover over that ghastly hole, whilst mother held our noses and we struggled to piss, like..like.." His hand stirred the air as he sought an apt image. "..Like lunatics making water through a strait-jacket," he finally said. He flushed slightly. "Sometimes I hid a water pistol between the flies of my trousers and just *pretended* to do the necessary. You understand - it kept mother happy?"

He broke off and accelerated as a car, which had hung on our tail for the past twenty minutes, tried to overtake in front of an oncoming vehicle. After much horn-honking and light-flashing Fabrice forced the nippy Clio to pull back behind our galumphing Deux Chevaux. Satisfied he'd won the set, if not the match, he resumed the dawdling speed essential to the telling of any good tale.

"One day poor mother could take it no more. It was during the war in Algeria, you know? The hole hadn't been emptied for eight months, so she decided to send for the local workman to do the job." He wiped his forehead. "Even now I remember it all so vividly! Mother barricaded the house like we were at war ourselves. All the shutters were tight closed, all the doors double-locked. I remember she told us bacteria were like invisible insects who could fly into the house through even the tiniest cracks."

Beset by an absolute imperative to demonstrate, Fabrice removed both hands from the wheel and gave a febrile flutter. I gasped as the car veered towards the ditch.

"She hung garlic at the windows and painted crosses on all the doors," he cried, catching the wheel at the very last moment.

His technique certainly worked wonders. Half asleep a moment before, I sat bolt upright now, listening to his every word.

"My brother and I crept up into the attic and removed a couple of roof tiles so we could watch. We saw the workman arrive dressed like something from Outer Space. We saw him take out his biggest spade and lever at the lid of the black hole. We saw the lid slowly, slowly creak open as the grass split away. And then we saw.."

Fabrice broke off and rammed his foot down, hard. The Clio was right up alongside us. I could see hair sprouting from the driver's nostrils. In a puff of fumes he was gone, leaving Fabrice waving an angry finger of derision. "Bloody maniac. Shouldn't be allowed on the road," he ranted.

"Well ?" I said a trifle breathlessly. "So what did you see?"

"See where?" he said absently. He was staring balefully at the empty road.

"In the black hole. What happened?"

"Oh that!" He chuckled and scratched his nose. To tell the truth I didn't see anything. You see I was so petrified by it all I jumped back and let go of the stepladder I was holding and m brother fell off the wall and broke his leg. He ever would tell me what he saw. But I know he had nightmares for years afterwards." He chuckled again. "Serves him right the little tyke!"

At Chatillon-sur-Indre we decided to stop for a bite to eat, and that's when we knew we were really in the countryside. It was only nine in the evening, but the local restaurateurs seemed to take it as a personal insult that we should expect food at such a 'late' hour.

We walked the dank streets, pushing open steamy doors on near-empty rooms and eavesdropping snippets of boastful, bleary conversation. Finally a gruff barman, behind a tiny bar bathed in excruciating green neon, took pity and agreed to make us a *Jambon-beurre.*' From a bin under the bar he extracted a limp baguette, chopped it in half with a knife the size of a miniature machete, and assaulted it with butter. Then the machete struck up and carved a hunk from a hanging ham. The meat was spanked firmly between two jaws of bread, sprinkled with a fistful of toad-backed gherkins, slapped together and after a thump for good measure, *voilà!* There was our sandwich. All done without washing hands, or donning gloves or any of the rest of those effeminate, germ-conjuring rituals which Europe was always trying to impose over here.

"Look at this place. I don't ask for grants do I?" He suddenly bawled at two old men hunkered over the bar.

Like a couple of toy dogs the two aged heads swung a solemn, 'no'.

"Want money for nothing. Plant fields of crops an' just leave 'em to rot." The barman's lips puckered in distaste. "They're crazy I tell you!" He tapped his forehead in disgust. "Crazy!" he muttered again.

There was a long silence, broken only by the habitual din of a football match on the big screen T.V. Chewing a nicotine-stained fingernail the barman watched the ball bounce back and forth for a moment and then with a sudden air of resolution he wiped his hands on an apron strained over his belly like risen dough, opened the fridge and fished out a couple of lettuce leaves and solemnly decorated our sandwiches.

"Look at his face," whispered Fabrice, who was watching the man with fascinated horror. "He's as white as my great grandfather's cadaver. Do you think he ever steps out from behind his bar?"

The barman had seized a bottle of wine. With practiced thumb he flicked off the plastic cork and slopped the acid beverage into two, smeary glasses. After mopping up the overspill with a sponge as gray as his face, he scrabbled behind one ear and recuperated a half-smoked Gitane cigarette which he lit, filling the room with smoke. A deft flick of wrist and ash told us to take our place at a table in the gloomy restaurant.

Reluctantly we quit the cosy ring of life round the bar and headed for our dismal table. It struck me I'd once read that France had more bars per square kilometre than any other country in

Europe and I wondered what was the point if, at 10pm on a Saturday night, they were all as empty as this one?

In the restaurant there were a half-dozen tables decked with oil cloths representing lurid scenes of dead pheasants and butchered boar. "Huntsman's' pornography," said Fabrice with a ghastly leer. We huddled near a cast iron Godin stove, which hacked and bubbled like an Opium smoker. A long pipe rose at a crazy angle and emptied smoke via a hole in the ceiling. "The modern adventure isn't a question of distance anymore. It's a question of depth," said Fabrice.

I nodded, struck by the idea. "This place is the living proof that you don't need to go far to be an explorer," I agreed.

Someone flicked a switch and the room was bathed in neon light. "Haven't they heard of mood lighting?" I joked feebly .

"It all depends on your mood. I should think it's a perfect light for alcoholics and people with other nasty addictions," said Fabrice. "It's probably pretty good for rampant psychopaths and mad axe murderers as well," he added as a gloomy afterthought.

A stocky waiter swooped in out of nowhere. He tapped the zinc with a curved fingernail to attract the barman's attention. "I'm telling you they can snuff it for all the Government care!" he bawled.

"Moi-je-te-dis! Moi-je-te-dis! No wonder they're nicknamed *'ch'ti'*, the northerners. They're always saying, *'Moi ch'ti! Moi ch'ti!'"* mocked Fabrice.

The waiter flung out a dramatic arm. "I tell you the farmers can snuff it for all the Government care! I know a bloke who works all the hours God sends, *AND..*" His voice climbed to cover an interruption. "..*AND* he still can't make ends meet! He's lucky to clear 700 francs a month, the poor bugger. They force him to take out loans to buy bigger and better machinery. Hah! Do you know where he gets clothes for his wife and kids? From the Red Cross, that's where!" His mouth screwed tight as if he'd like to spit at this ultimate insult to working man.

Fabrice nudged me. "Ask for the sandwiches," he whispered.

"Ask for them yourself!" I hissed. But neither of us did ask. We were townies. We were used to polite voices and tight gestures dictated by limited city space, and all this *sturm and drang* was really quite bewildering. So we just cowered hungrily in the shadows, listening to the Godin hoick and gargle, and the broad-accented French blaring round us like fog.

"Keep up with progress they tell him. Progress for who, I ask you?" the waiter trumpeted on. "He'll work all his life just to pay off his debts and then he'll snuff it. They've got him by the.." He

15

broke off and scooped an explicit hand towards his genitals. And then he sighed and - to my utter astonishment - as the murmurs of angry agreement reached their crescendo, he just shrivelled like half-baked dough. *"Qu'est-ce que tu veut?* he muttered and outspread palms clearly signalled his defeat. *"On n'y peut rien* - there's nothing we can do," he said. He sighed again, scratched his flies vigorously then served us our sandwiches.

It was the first time I was to hear that phrase, but it was not to be the last. How familiar it became in future months. Over and over again I heard it, in the mouths of young and old alike: *"On y peut rien* - there's nothing we can do."

I came to recognize it as a leitmotif of modern rural life. It seemed to encapsulate the heavy pessimism of communities whose existence was defined by battles with Mother Nature and with 'them up there in Paris': battles that they never seemed to win. *"On y peut rien,,"* they said. "There's nothing we can do."

And behind those words, like an echo, I seemed to hear another voice muttering: "Nothing ever changes, so nothing ever will."

CHAPTER TWO

Crossing the Loire is an important psychological moment. France's most famous river is said to signal the climatic divide between north and south. 'It can be raining on one side and bright sunshine on the other', a popular saying goes, so when we reached the river we stopped the car and got out to see if this was true. And as we stood there, admiring the vast expanse of water tickled by a pale finger of moonlight, it seemed to me I could feel the balmy air. "The south is wonderful," I proclaimed as I clambered back into the car. "It's the shrill chatter of crickets on hot summer nights. The sound of amorous frogs grunting love songs from the cool refuge of their ponds. The south is honey-sweet odours of Jasmine and meaty scents of Sage and Thyme. The south is passion, with a capital 'P'. It's the very opposite to northern indifference. Flowers burn hot with colour and food strikes the taste buds like an iron glove challenging them to do duel. Even

17

before eating you're visually replete: satiated at the mere sight of juice-popping tomatoes soaked in olive oil and scattered with chunks of garlic..."

My voice faded. I was far away. I was lounging on a bamboo-covered terrace, surrounded by houses whose whitewashed walls were bedecked with peeled green shutters and trimmed with crimson hollyhocks. I was nursing a deliciously chilled goblet of rosé in my sticky palm whilst Wisteria waved wistful purple tendrils out of the drowned depths of secret gardens at me. I could hear sun-drunk bees buzzing with bliss and feel delicious, drowsy heat coating my skin like varnish. "South!" I sighed.

Fabrice snorted loudly. "South my backside!" he cried. "La Charente isn't the Côte d'Azur, you know. In winter it gets bitter cold."

I sulked until we got to a walled toy-town perched high above the Charente river, called Angoulême. It was way past midnight and our clumsy vehicle lumbered through the dozing streets like a dinosaur on stilts. Mercifully we quit the cobbled conurbation in seconds and we were heading for La Rochfoucauld. 'Foucauld's rock' was even smaller: just one main street and a few dozen shops huddled beneath a castle which looked like it had been filched from Blois. After La Rochfoucauld our main road fizzled out completely. We were on a country lane following signs for Montemboeuf.

Branches of crinkled oak leaves, whose forests bordered either side of the pot-holed road we bounced along, whipped our windscreen viciously. In the whistling dark it seemed as if we were the only souls alive. From time to time a long slope of roof appeared, surrounded by slumber-struck cows, only to be whisked away again by gloom. From time to time a light shone out from a distant farmhouse, but it's homely flicker only emphasized the lonely night. I felt like a character out of one of Thomas Hardy's novels: I was Tess, alone, on Egdon heath. "There is more to Heaven and Earth, Horatio," I said solemnly

Fabrice stared at me. "I beg your pardon?" he said.

I translated the essence of Shakespeare's idea to him. He just grunted. For him, it was perfectly *obvious* that there was more to Heaven and Earth than was dreamt of in our philosophies.

We wallowed on along the bumpy track. A meagre slip of moon dodged between dark shreds of cloud and cast shadows of frantic boughs across the road ahead of us - they looked like arms trying to wave us down. In the shifting, gusting obscurity a star ignited and was instantly extinguished. It was a wild night. A night for brigands and ruffians, footpads and bloodthirsty, cut-throat villains. My blood was racing now – I realised I was petrified. Then I understood what was making me so uneasy. It was the lack of light. That aniseed-coloured, street lamp glow which is a constant presence in cities, was absent here. All the anxiety I hadn't allowed myself to feel before leaving, started to well up inside me. The surrounding blackness seemed like the mirror of my future. All was dark before me. I was heading for the unknown..

"MERDE!"

There was a harsh squeal of brakes. The car slewed across the road, on a carpet of wet leaves, and slithered to a standstill with its bonnet just inches from an imposing oak trunk. The engine's bark was replaced by the wind's breath and we watched in awe as a deer pranced across our path and vanished under a low net of boughs.

"Is there a wildlife park near here, or something?" I said inanely.

Fabrice laughed raucously. "The forests here are full of deer. And partridges." He licked his lips. "And wild boar."

It struck me I'd lived in towns for too long. The notion of hairy, black pigs with big, pointed tusks roaming free near roads seemed quite archaic to me.

We arrived at Mouzon along a road stippled with sharp blades of grass that had pierced the tarmac like a colander.. We stopped an instant on the brow of the hill, cut the motor and stared down at the slumbering village. In the centre sat a mediaeval church, squat as a brooding hen, and a half-a-dozen houses clustered round it like new born chicks. A cow mooed forlornly, then coughed like a geriatric. The air was full of the smell of fresh-hoed earth, and rotted apples and mouldy hay.

Almost out of petrol now we freewheeled down the slope, ghosted round a bend and glided to a standstill. Above us loomed two storeys of bulging granite, covered in Virginia creeper. Left to itself for decades the enterprising plant had sneaked shoots under the warped shutters and it's tiny fingers were busily prising the wood away from the windows. 'Time' - which meant 'money' where I came from - seemed to be a negligible quantity here. 'Whether it's in this century, or the next, I'll get those shutters off their hinges in the end," the creeper seemed to say. I stared up at the ancient abode. There was something familiar about it. It was like something I dreamt of, once, in a long distant past

Wind rocked the boughs of a big old pine tree by the buckled front gate and birds, dozing in it's feathered branches, turned uneasily and tweeted softly in their sleep. Behind us in the thick oak forest an owl hooted, and from somewhere deep in the heart of our new home another one tooted an answer.

"I'll open up," mouthed Fabrice.

"O.K," I breathed back. Instinctively we were whispering.

Fabrice flourished a key the size and shape of an old warming pan and - after tearing away the fingers of creeper which had already got to work on the immense oak door - slotted it into the cavernous lock. The door gave inward with the wail of a fleeing poltergeist. How long was it since it was last opened? I wondered. I shuddered, beset with visions of bare mud floors and soiled straw mattresses. But there was no time for further reflection. In time-honoured tradition Fabrice had swept me up in his arms and was carrying me over the threshold. "Welcome to your new home," he said.

Dozens of light-starved, bulge-eyed spiders dived for cover as we entered. Their antique webs, which hung across the doorway like lace, burst asunder covering my hair with a fragile veil. I thought of Miss Haversham and her wedding one and hoped this wasn't a bad omen Then the door banged shut and the light flickered on and the first thing I saw – to my immense relief - was an inside toilet. Set bang in the middle of the draughty corridor which cut right through the centre of the house, it was hard to

22

miss. Deeply traumatized by the 'black hole', it was as if Fabrice's family had put this modern, porcelain miracle firmly in evidence. I imagined it must be an emotionally charged symbol for them. Like a war memorial, or a lover's framed letter, this inside toilet stood as a constant reminder of all the horrors they would never again be forced to suffer.

There were two, vast rooms downstairs. To the left of the family's plumbing icon the cruel light of a naked bulb revealed a kitchen with crumbling stone walls and beams the size of tree trunks. In the centre stood a farm table, with space to seat twelve, and two long benches. There were chestnut floorboards that had been splintered by the jaws of - what looked to be giant - rats and opposite the table at knee-level there was a stone basin whose rim was worn thin from centuries of pummelling and scrubbing. Just above it jutted a small window, called an *'oeil de boeuf'*, which Fabrice, yawning, told me served the dual purpose of providing light to lather by and a hole to sling the lather through after.

I opened the door - situated to the right of the omnipresent toilet monument - and briefly discovered the lounge, before being sucked backwards by a draught which tore down the chimney, snatched the door from my hand and slammed it in my face. Using two hands I opened the door again, cautiously this time, and this time it dealt me a giant whack on the backside, propelling me into the middle of the room. Rubbing my sore rear end I gazed around in dazed wonder. This room was big enough to contain my entire Greenwich flat - the fireplace on its own looked big enough to live in! I imagined Fabrice's ancestors clad in rustic smocks huddled round the fire to warm their work-calloused hands, roasting chestnuts, cobbling socks and spinning yarns as the long winter raged outside – and I wondered what they'd have made of the centrally-situated toilet.

Yawning now, we clambered up the rough oak staircase, (just behind the toilet) slid in socks across the parquet bedroom floor, climbed up into the tall-legged boat-bed, rolled ourselves in a musty clubber of goose-down quilts, snuffled the sour odour of wood smoke which seemed to have impregnated the peeling plaster walls and slid into a sweet, dreamless sleep.

"Bang!"

What was that? I jerked upright. There was a brief scuffle and then silence. Heart pounding I lay in the narrow cot imagining all sorts of malevolent spooks and listening to the roof timbers groaning like an OAP with lumbago, the cat squealing as a rat nipped his muzzle in the kitchen, creepers scratching the window like imploring fingers and Fabrice, dead to the world, snoring like a blunt old chainsaw.

Alone in the darkness the folly of our act took on a startling clarity. Both dedicated socialisers we'd come to a hamlet where the youngest resident was in his sixties and bedtime coincided with the setting sun. From well-paid jobs in the city we'd come to an area where unemployment was rife and those who had a job were lucky to earn the minimum wage. It was difficult not to wonder if we'd done the right thing.

I was apprehensive about our future, I was scared of spooks, but I was a lot more terrified of the ghosts I'd fled. Of the phantoms which haunt the recess of our minds – the ghosts of envy, bitterness and regret which would have haunted my days if I hadn't done what I really wanted to do. If I hadn't had the courage to start a new life.

Down in the kitchen Typhus, the cat who'd spent most of his life in an overheated Versailles flat, was having his first taste of freedom and finding it bitter-sweet. I finally fell asleep again to the sound of his mournful howling at the moon.

CHAPTER THREE

Somewhere above thick layers of sleep I heard a tinny bell chiming. Birds joined in tweeping wildly, then a couple of cows decided to get in on the al fresco concert and started blowing like love-struck elephants.

Bounding out of bed, barefoot, I slung back the creaking shutters and admired the jumble of ochre roofs. They were the same colour as the cows grazing in the surrounding fields and they steamed, just like the bovine's flanks did, in an early morning mist. Previous nights fears seemed a million miles away now. Re-hashed, heated up and served on a brand new day the unknown was a dish which suddenly seemed very appealing. "So this is Mouzon?" I thought as I stared down into the dusty, empty street - this was the main avenue and it was dotted with beret-sized cow pats. I watched a frail old gent - shaken by a high wind I guessed he'd brewed in a homemade still - totter past the church and vanish into a dank-walled house. Then the road was empty again. There were half a dozen houses in varying states of decay on either side. A mud splattered signpost informed me we were 15 kilometres from the nearest large village and double that from any major centre.

A cock crowed from the house opposite, urging the day to carry him forward to the moment when he'd get his bowl of grain. Hens made cooing baby noises as they rolled up feathers like elderly bathers and took dips in their individual dust baths. There was a smell of cow dung in the crisp air and the wooden odour of damp tarmac and a rear tang of rotted apples. A gaggle of pigeons appeared, sweeping the air up behind them in dry brush strokes and carrying it high above a line of lime trees, whose amputated branches stretched like lepers fists to the healing sun. The heavens were as blue as the roof of a Greek Orthodox church and twice as distant, and an inky line of '*Massif Centrale*' foothills on the horizon seemed like the earth's final outpost before this wide blue yonder sky.

For a long blessed instant there was silence, then a dog let out a blood-curdling howl and another followed suite and soon the village was one long, deafening bawl. Over the hubbub came a loud honking and the squeal of tyres. I heard voices raised in agitation. "Has there been an accident?" I asked Fabrice.

He snored peacefully, totally unperturbed by the racket outside. I prodded him. "Is there going to be a fight?" I bellowed in his ear..

"Iss the bakers van," he finally condescended to groan. I was assailed by visions of elderly oafs battling to get the first baguette. "But why on earth are they shouting like that - do they hate each other, or what?" I asked, bewildered.

The goose quilt rode up and crawled across the mattress like the Lochness monster on the run from another 'B' movie. "They do mostly hate each other, but that's not why they're shouting," Fabrice sniggered.

"Then why..?"

The quilt jiggered silently and a cloud of dust motes rose into the sunlit air. "It's because they're nearly all stone deaf," he guffawed. "That's why they're shouting like that!"

Undeterred I hung out of the window to get a glimpse of my new neighbours. The first thing that struck me was that they were all women, all over sixty, all had walking sticks and ear horns and - to make the resemblance even spookier - they all wore hairnets!

As I eyed the swelling crowd a voice started carking somewhere in the back of mind. After some rooting I traced it to Fabrice's mother. "Ze trouble wiz ze women in ze countryside is zat zey just let zemselves go," she was lecturing through a pout of freshly applied lipstick. For an uncanny second it was as if she was standing right beside me, staring with me at the motley crowd below. I could almost smell her very particular skin odour - which had been modified by years of buying cheap versions of expensive perfumes, to plain chemical stink. "Zis is what will happen to you. It is ze destiny of all women who dare to bury themselves in ze 'eart of ze French countryside," I heard her croak and just then my gaze fell on an imposing column of flesh, rolled up in a stylish horsehair blanket and totally devoid of the usual waist/breast indentations,. and much as I hated to admit it I could see she had a point.

'Shapeless', as I dubbed her, was chatting with a wild-eyed, toothless octogenarian who, despite a bewildering choice of candidates, I instantly dubbed 'granny'. All flapping arms and red-cheeks 'Shapeless seemed to be doing an impression of Leonardo da Vinci trying to convince his mates he would, one day, fly, whilst, visibly unimpressed, 'Granny' was doing a try-out for Hamlet. "To be or not to be?" she seemed to cry, as her gnarled fingers clawed

29

the sky. "To be or not to be..?" Oh *merde!* She'd forgotten the rest and was stamping her foot in anger.

Dragging on a pair of trousers, hair stuck up like a Crested Cockatoo, Fabrice descended into the thick of it to buy a *'Couronne'* of bread. As he approached the fringes of the crowd there was an excited swell of babble. "Adi!" I heard someone cry.

"Comment va-ti?" said another. Then he was swallowed up in an exuberant sea of nylon rollers.

The women, who'd been chatting in thick gobs of local patois, spoke French now - which they called *'Français'* as if it was a foreign language - for Fabrice's benefit. "How are your mamma and papa?" they cooed - as if he was in short britches and not pushing 40 - and some of the hardier ones even evoked memories of his antics in nappies. Having elucidated certain mysteries (like how his mother had managed to get her claws into a boyfriend who was less than half her age, or why his sister, who was expecting her second child, was still unwed), the conversation, inevitably, turned to health.

Père Buissard next door had just had a third heart operation at the grand old age of 85. "And he still drives his Deux Chevaux van!" exclaimed Granny, who was his, third, wife.

"But he drives it on the wrong side of the road," pointed out an angular female whose horn-rimmed glasses were so steamed-up she looked as if she'd just stepped out of a Turkish bath.

Granny sniffed loudly. "The important thing is his will to live, not stupid little errors like which side of the road he drives on," came her scornful response. She looked around her seeking agreement. There were a few, vague murmurs, but most of the crowd had switched channels and were listening to 'Shapeless' telling the tale of her Ghastly Tumour. "As big as this!" she shrieked and she flung out her arms like a fisherman describing 'the one that got away'.

"And what about my bowels?" yelled Granny, in a desperate attempt to make a come back. But her bowels were a non-starter, so she pulled out her trump card. "I remember when they dug out my cataracts," she howled. Unfortunately that old chestnut had been roasted on the fire of local gossip a hundred times, too, so she fell back on Fabrice. "He used a thing like a soup spoon," I made out before her voice sank to a confidential mutter. When Fabrice blenched and tried to pull away she grabbed his arm and leaned in closer. "All pink and mushy," I heard her whisper as she scraped her withered cheeks at him, like a dog going after a bone.

Shapeless, meanwhile, was onto another winner with what she called her 'total', or, 'the descent of my yooterus'. "They cut me there! And there! And there!" she cried, savagely quartering the air. "And now I have nothing down there," she added, with a faint note of triumph.

"And did *HE* ever notice?" piped up a leathery gnome who seemed to be the crowd's token male.

'Shapeless' scabrous response was drowned out in general mirth and during this brief hiatus the baker suggested that someone might like to buy his bread, since it was the reason - *n'est-ce pas?*, - for this impromptu little gathering. Unfortunately for him someone had just chimed in with that ultimate conversation-stopper: 'He's not got long to live' and bread was pushed to the bottom of the menu once more. Defeated, the baker leant back against a shelf of piping hot croissants to wait a little longer.

"Who?" came a dozen, prurient whispers.

"The butcher," came the hoarse reply.

"All the better, the old robber! That way I won't have to pay his bill." said Steamy Specs.

There were a few uncertain cackles and then a general sigh went up. "*C'est la misère, té,*" Granny launched, like a password.

32

"*On n'y peut rien,*" came the well-worn response and this time, when the baker ventured to make his presence known, Steamy Specs was shoved to the front of the queue. A few moments later she made off down the road clutching an armful of bread to her pigeon breast. "Ahh, that one," someone exclaimed as soon as she was out of earshot. "She has the *cuisse légère!*" Which phrase I translated as 'the light thigh' and wondered if it had anything to do with that other puzzling French expression, '*mon cul c'est du poulet*', which is used to indicate incredulity and bizarrely translates as: 'My bottom is chicken'.

I was soon to be enlightened. "She goes into the woods with all of the men," I heard Shapeless explain to Fabrice.

I stared in wonder after the pair of thin shanks shambling off down the road. She wore transparent pop socks which had worked their way down her hairy legs and dangled there like a shaggy membrane, she had curlers in her hair and to complement this arousing accoutrement she wore a faded blue housecoat and a pair of welly boots lopped off at the ankles. She was about as appetising as Gérard Départdieu in drag, yet for these women, I realised, she was Mouzon's answer to Mata-Hari.

33

Granny nudged Fabrice in the ribs. "She'll be after you," she cackled and Fabrice, who'd just got his colour back, paled once more.

We took breakfast on the smooth granite step in front of the house, which had sucked up heat from the late-season sun and warmed our buttocks like a stone radiator. Fabrice carved hunks from the 'Couronne' - a loaf of bread, the size and shape of a bathing ring – and we dotted the chunks with globs of icy butter then dipped them into our bowls of coffee. Pale circles of butter floated to the surface like oiled smoke rings and the air around us was filled with a comfortingly fragrant steam.

After chomping for a while I noticed the leathery gnome screeching back and forth on his moped. I admired the rakish angle of his beret and commented on the stylish pair of cow horns he'd fixed to the moped's handlebars. Fabrice informed me this was Dédé, an ageing bachelor-boy who looked after the village cows and was known to be a staunch communist. Between large bites Fabrice explained that Dédé had never, in his life, been further than 30 miles from Mouzon, except for once when he'd lit out for Russia on a package tour to seek out his formaldehyde hero, Lenin.

"He'll do that all day," Fabrice told me as Dédé chundered past once more. "Something happened to him after Russia. Something just snapped. Some say it was the Vodka, but I think it was Lenin. Apparently when he got back, he didn't speak to anyone for several days and then he finally confessed to Père Buissard. He said that Lenin had looked like one of the blow-up dolls he bought at the local sex-shop and it had come as a terrible shock."

I nodded sympathetically. Discovering you'd spent half your life worshipping a cut-price substitute for copulation must come as a heavy blow.

A bell tolled out and its tinny chime vied with bees who were having several thousand winks in the creeper above our heads. "For whom the bell tolls," I said solemnly.

"It tolls for Claude," said Fabrice. He sniggered. "They call him the *'petit fou'* – which roughly translates as, 'the little nutter'. He's Dédé's drinking pal. The two of them made a bet that Claude couldn't get up each morning and ring that bell."

As he spoke the tolling stretched into one, long, roll and Dédé chundered past, face red and beret askew. He was heading for the church. "When did they make this bet ?"I asked.

Fabrice scratched his head. "Sometime back in the 1940's as far as I know," he said.

Dédé reached the square, threw down his steed and started climbing the bell tower steps, two at a time.

"And has he won the bet?" I asked.

Fabrice snorted loudly. "He's won the bet alright. The only trouble is the *fou* is so drunk from the night before, nine-times-out-of-ten he goes to sleep, hanging from the bell like a giant bat, and poor old Dédé has to climb up there and pull him down."

After breakfast I left Fabrice to scrub and wax the old house down whilst I set out to explore, not with the rose-tinted gaze of a visitor but with the unforgiving scrutiny of one who was here to stay.

With it's ball-size rooms, belly-thick walls, and thigh-wide beams there was no doubt that the place had charm - it was just the basic amenities that were lacking. It was only late September but already it was bitterly, freezing cold and I'd have traded a spadeful of atmosphere for just spoonful of heat from my old Greenwich flat. With nose and fingers the colour of a gaudy tricolour I poked around the kitchen seeking warmth only to discover the only - highly ornate - stove which was the size and shape of a large matchbox. "Winter's going to be fun," I thought.

A gas oven stood opposite the stove and this item made my heart sink even further. Some sinister hand had scrawled, 'Danger', across it in blood. I shuddered, wondering if this was some murder victim's cryptic last message, or just a reference to the oven. On closer inspection the 'blood' revealed itself to be lipstick and the 'sinister hand' to be Fabrice's mother's. The oven was still a nightmare, however, and I stared gloomily at its rust-incrusted rings, instantly dumping fantasies of fab-food parties for new-found friends. I'd be lucky to get a boiled egg out of this thing.

Just above the gas oven there was another, equally awesome, spectacle. Some DIY freak from another century - or planet! - had rigged up what had to be the first ever model of a gas immersion heater. This pathetic collector's item clung to a blackened wall which should have aroused my suspicions. But I was so relieved to discover there was hot water, I didn't stop to think. Still pondering upon the marvels of progress which had made this pitiful contraption obsolete – probably before it had hatched its first flicker - I connected the blue bottle of butane gas, lit the pilot flame, turned on the hot water tap and..Nothing. The water was icy cold. 'Don't do it,' moaned a voice in my inner ear. But I was as blithely obtuse as an actor from 'Blair Witch' and I wanted my hot water, so I bent down and peered inside the rusting box waving a flaming match. I was puzzled by an ominous rattle which sounded like a pea speeding down a high velocity peashooter and I was still puzzled when a huge ball of flame shot out and sent me reeling back to butt against a shelf, conveniently rigged at head height by the same DIY enthusiast, and disappear beneath a pile of soot .

This was the moment Fabrice chose to pop his head round the door. "Who on earth is burning hair like that? It's disgusting," I heard him mutter. He caught sight of me and started back in surprise. "Why are you messing around in all that soot. Can't you see I've just cleaned in here?" He said angrily. He stopped, abruptly. " Well, I never!" he said peering at me in wonder. "We've been together for over a year now and this is the first time I've ever noticed you had bald eyes."

The ball of fire seemed to have decongested the heater so I took a much-needed shower. Since the cubicle was set right next to the toilet it was, of course, slap-bang in the middle of the corridor and basic privacy was assured by a thin cotton curtain. Pulling the curtain aside I fished a couple of stiff rodents out of the basin and stepped, lash-less, naked and shivering under the jet of scalding water. Which instantly ran cold. I stepped out of the shower. The water ran hot again. I hopped back under the stream. It sputtered and went icy cold. Out in the corridor Fabrice whistled like a canary as he waxed and scrubbed enough to make any mother - even his own, mad one – proud and every now and then he opened the front door wide. As I hopped frenetically in and out of the ice-cold/scalding dribble, draughts tore along the corridor and flipped up the flimsy curtain to reveal my naked body half way into, or half way out of, the shower, to half the village. It struck me as a novel, if embarrassing, way to be introduced to my new neighbours.

After a quick rub down with a mouldering towel, I was ready for the second part of my house tour, but when I opened the door of the lounge I nearly slammed it shut and went back to bed. Bad taste, I realised surveying the unspeakable horror of pink fluffy chairs sporting pom-poms, neo-classic plastic mirrors with tassels on and a selection of pea-green/orange-glo sofas which would've made even the most hardened 70's fan wince, was just as good a way of getting equal with one's enemies, as any other. If I'd wondered about the odd tensions which circulated in Fabrice's family I had found the key. This living room furniture revealed the murderous hate they nurtured for each other, far more clearly than mere words could have done. There could be no doubt of the sadistic intentions of successive tides of twisted family members who, in receding, had deposited such a ghastly bladder wrack of embittered furnishings upon these country shores. Children and dogs, who'd obviously detested this furniture as much as their parents and masters, had done their level best to contribute. Overly ornate chair legs were liberally stamped with '*Tou-tou*' the terrier's needle fangs. Dear little Marie-Hélène had torn the stuffing out of most of the sofas and younger brother, 'Jean-Mi', had had a field day with felt tips on the Formica tables.

The *Prix de Guerre*, however, had to go to an elder sister who'd hit on the horrid idea of Bernard Buffet paintings. I was brought to an abrupt halt by the mawkish mask of a clown tacked up over the fireplace. It was such a wretched sight I felt like bursting into huge, wracking sobs. But Big Sis wasn't going to let me off so lightly. Cunningly hung on a plaster wall of such horrendous scrofulousness the eye couldn't fail to be drawn to it, was another Buffet in the linear shape of a fishing port which seemed to teem with the bodies of everybody who was ever lost at sea. Still reeling from the blows dealt me in this aesthetic Dirty War, I edged out into the corridor and bumped into Fabrice, who informed me that Monsieur Buffet had been a manic depressive. I can't say I was terribly surprised.

Out in the hall I discovered that the DIY freak from-outer-space had been busy again, this time with the wiring. Eyeing the pot-noodle of wires, terminating in bared bulbs and metal sockets, which festooned the corridor like Halloween at Christmas, it occurred to me if he'd wired up his own house in the same way he must have died quite a while ago and had a very cheap cremation. It took only the smallest flight of fancy to picture Fabrice's diabolical family conniving to get each other to switch on a light whilst standing under the shower, or reach up to change the bulb in that naked socket with one hand dipped in soapy water..

Fabrice zipped past with a feather duster, interrupting my reveries. "Well? So what do you think of your new home then?" he asked.

I thought an instant. "There's no heating to speak of and just enough hot water to spit at, and there are sadistic decorative elements and electrical facilities which would be the envy of Death Row," I said slowly.

Fabrice raised an expectant eyebrow. "So?" he said.

I grinned at him. "So, I love it!" I said.

41

CHAPTER FOUR

We were at the end of a boggy track when a clutch of snarling dogs with sunken flanks sprang out of nearby undergrowth. Fabrice waved a rotten branch and they made off howling. Opposite us was another boggy track, which looked exactly like the one we'd been following for the past two hours and led through exactly the same scenery of tea-stained fields and forests bristling with oak, and pine. There wasn't a single house in sight. We were lost, in France, in the rain.

"It's this way, I tell you," Fabrice said for the hundredth time. We stood and squabbled a bit, then shared our last handful of boiled chestnuts, squeezing the sweet gobs into our hungry mouths like toothpaste.

The air was sour with odours of wet wood and pine needles and metallic rain. Our cheeks had lost their townie sheen and were mottled like ripe apples. To the touch of effort-swollen fingers my skin was as smooth as porcelain. Several large hawks circled above us. Two badgers swayed past not even bothering to look at us.

"We should complain," said Fabrice *à propos* of nothing. He held out a palmful of chestnuts. "When you think that, not so long ago, this was all that people had to live off," he said.

"If we go on turning in circles like this it might be all we have to live off, too," I said moodily. I was exhausted. We'd been tramping for hours in this wilderness. It would've seemed tame enough to the wild men of Borneo, but to me it was like thickest jungle. I took a few, deep breaths and admired the shaggy needles draped like a tatty Afghan coat over the branches of a nearby pine. For the first time in my life, here beneath these centurion trees and far from the city's madding crowds, it struck me that there was something rotten in the state of Denmark. "There is something rotten in the state of Denmark," I said solemnly.

Fabrice sniffed the air. "Perhaps it is the mushrooms?" he hazarded

"This world is rotten," I cried. I pointed to a slug. "Don't you see that even this poor, humble slug makes more sense than I do, because he is in touch with something that is real, eternal and immutable?"

Fabrice scratched his head. "He's in touch with a lot of mud," he said.

"Don't you see our human world is out of kilter?" I bellowed.

"Err..."

"Don't you see we're less adapted to our environment than any other species and yet we Lord it over all the others. That we live in an era which is obsessed with communication and yet we can't even communicate with each other. That we keep wanting 'more' and 'better' and faster.."

"..And getting stupider, and fatter and slower?"

"Exactly!"

"Well if you put it like that, I suppose I do."

I shrugged. The rain had slackened and a ray of sunshine in the rubbed-out sky set raindrops chiming in all the cobwebs - even the slug sparkled like brushed copper. The world looked less tragic now.

We set off again, refreshed. Further along the track we saw a tatty ball of feathers struggling in the mud. Two hawks swooped down and jabbed at it with fierce, curved beaks. We ran up with our sticks and chased them off. "The thing about nature is that it's often so cruel," said Fabrice as he gathered up the frightened duckling and stuffed it in his jacket pocket.

"And human beings aren't?" I said.

A few yards more and we finally came across 'civilisation' in the shape of five, or six, houses in various spectacular stages of decay. Great beams had fallen inward staving holes in massive walls and ivy had stepped in to lend a hand – or, rather, several thousand helping fingers – with destruction work. Two of the houses were nothing more than piles of rubble and seemed to have dragged their roofs down around them like shrouds to hide their crippled shame. We paused for breath in front of a granite arch which looked like one of Gandalf's doorways into the Dark Mountain. "1572", we read. Fabrice whistled. "Talk about the place that time forgot," he said.

I nodded in similar disbelief. Only think of it: a whole village of antique beams, stone fireplaces and original features left to go to rack and ruin - why, it was utter sacrilege to my Brit-bred sentiments!

We clambered over the rubble and poked our noses inside the pots and pans of blasted kitchens and up the staggering chimneys of imploded bedrooms. It was hard to believe that anyone had really lived here. "None of the locals want to buy these old places. They grew up between damp old walls like these. They know all about dark kitchens filled with smoke and the difficulties of cooking on wood-burning stoves," Fabrice explained. "The rural past is recent history for them. It hasn't had time to get 'quaint', or *'recherché'* here like it has in so many other European countries," he added.

And it struck me as ironic. To think that, at a time when State-of-the-Art boutiques in major cities were hailing Lino and Formica as the height of fashion, French country dwellers were still yearning for these 'little luxuries' the first time around. No wonder they were perfectly happy to sell off their extraneous piles of rubble to those 'crazy English', or more recently Dutch and Germans, who lived outside in caravans for years on end whilst they carried out their careful renovations. It occurred to me in years to come rural France would probably feel the full, ironic weight of waking up one day to find that most of its own heritage was firmly in the hands of 'outsiders'.

A glabrous wisp of smoke wriggled out of the loose-bricked chimney pot of a house which seemed marginally less ramshackle than the rest. Fabrice suggested we stop here and ask the way. We entered the courtyard. Chickens, geese and ducks splattered in a sea of mud stretching right up to the battered front door. Windows were thick with grime and curtains hung limp as rags and yet even here, amidst utter desolation, the superfluous urge to

she clouted him heartily on the back. "Come in!" she cried in a tone which brooked no refusal.

We were no longer strangers, we were *'du pays'*, and we had to the seal on this unexpected rekindling of love's old flame by joining with her in an ubiquitous *apéritif*.

CHAPTER FIVE

Stepping over a couple of Muscovy ducks and the body of her expiring cur, we followed Fabrice's new-found friend into a hot, airless kitchen. With the shutters tightly closed and the only light cast by a porcelain lamp and the glimmer of a crackling fire, it was like entering a Van Eycke oil painting where the colours have been worn by centuries into a uniform, sepia glose.

In the shadows which gathered at one end of the room I made out what looked to be a coffin on rat-nibbled legs, but when I asked Fabrice if this meant a recent decease he explained that it was the cherry wood *'Maie'*, where the older folk still stored their bread. There was also a tall, oak buffet, with a lid on it - which he told me was a *'Blutoir'* used for milling wheat to make flour - and three bucket-sized iron pans hung above a glittering, granite fireplace which he said were for roasting chestnuts. Tucked away in the snug beside the fire a short, fat gnome sat chipping away at a

chunk of wood. Dispensing with introductions our hostess pointed a blood-grimed finger at him. "Don't know much what use he is for.. Just look at him! Can't work, can't go out, can't even help me with the vegetable garden. Can't do anything 'cept chip away at bits of wood like a blasted woody-woodpecker.." She sighed heavily. "*On n'y peut rien*," she said.

The gnome glanced up from his chipping. In the fire's light his skin shone pearly white. "I can't go out in the daytime. It burns me up," he said and he pointed proudly at the brown patches which mapped his opalescent skin like a jigsaw puzzle. Our hostess bustled round the room bumping into chairs, fumbling over shelves and rootling through cupboards as she assembled an odd collection of tumblers. The Gnome winked at us and his left eyeball glittered like an old, glazed marble. "Mother's as blind as a bat," he said. Then he pointed to his own eye, as proud as if it were a medal. "I was hoeing a field when a stone flew up and *bang!*" He explained and he mimed an eye dangling from it's socket.

"Will you stop wind-bagging an' tell me if these are the right glasses?" our hostess nagged. She was checking them over with Braille-readers fingers and now she shoved them, one by one, into his face as they chivvied each other like Punch and Judy. 'Where did you put those biscuits?" she niggled.

"Where you said I should put them."

"Oh, no you didn't!"

"Oh, yes I did!"

She opened a cupboard and started fumbling around in it. Over her shoulder I caught a glimpse of crumpled prescriptions and pots of potions and powders and pills. I remembered a French doctor telling me that the French consumed more sedatives and tranquillisers than any of the other peoples of Europe. "Here in the countryside we prescribe thousands of drugs each year to depressed women," he'd told me.

"And what do the men do. Don't they get depressed?" I'd innocently asked.

"Oh they get depressed alright, but they don't generally bother with pills. Generally, they hang themselves. It's so much cheaper," came his breezy response.

Our hostess let out a triumphant cry now and plonked a bottle down on the table. The liquid inside was the colour and texture of motor oil and there was a thick silt at the bottom. A few new-potato-shaped brown lumps stirred uneasily, then settled. "Homemade prune liqueur," our hostess informed us, rubbing her grubby hands. She hauled out a tin of biscuits, opened it and clawed the contents like a miser.

The gnome shot upright and his chunk of wood fell to the floor with a clatter. "Biscuits - yum, yum, yum!" he screeched.

She glared at him as if he was guilty of some appalling breach of social etiquette. "They're not for you, they're for special occasions," she snapped slapping the lid back on the container.

As she did so I saw the price on the tin was in ancient French Francs. 'Such occasions must be rare', I thought.

She ushered us to take a seat at the long farm table and we sat on a hard bench, opposite the odd couple, doused in a shower of light from the central lamp. Fingers trembling with age, or reverence, our hostess served us the prune liqueur. The date on the bottle read '1961'. "These prunes were around when Johnny Hallyday still looked like a rock idol and not like his own replica from Madame Tussauds", I mused. It struck me that these prunes had seen the man on the moon and miniskirts and Gérard Départieu as a big, fat baby in nappies.

The juice trickled out sluggishly at first, then shot out in a long, shuddering spasm. Only when our glasses were full-to-overflowing did our hostess put down the bottle and fix us beadily. Her lips spread in a chilling, coquettish leer. "How old do you think I am?" she asked Fabrice. In the pitiless light of the central lamp her withered cheeks were as rutted as a ploughed field and dotted with stiff spikes of hair – it was the skin of a frostbitten cactus. As for her nose, it was a mass of warts and her chin hung down in pleats like a much-used Elizabethan ruff.

Fabrice didn't bat an eyelid. "Surely you're not more than a year over 40?" he said.

There was a noise like a drain being unblocked "Just like your dear old grandpa," she gurgled and she patted his cheek with a fond, blood-grimed paw, then turned to me. "Well?" she said. Her old fingers picked restlessly at the tablecloth

"Err, 85?" I hazarded.

"I'm 95," she crowed. "And him?"

She stuck a bony finger in the Gnome's chest. He sat puffed out in expectation, like a Robin in heavy snow. "I'm 76," he said, spoiling her game.

"He's never married. He's my son."

"Stayed with mother..."

"..all his life."

"Couldn't leave the poor thing..."

"..couldn't if he tried!" She snatched up the bottle again and started filling our overfilled glasses. The sticky liquid seeped out

56

over the rim and formed oily pools on the table cloth. "Made it myself," she told us again.

"Mother made it," the Gnome repeated dutifully. There was a soft 'pop' and several potato-shaped objects slid out of the bottle's neck and sank to the bottom of my glass. As if this was the signal she'd been waiting for, mother set down the bottle and swept up her tumbler. "*A votre santé!*" she said, gaily clinking it against our own.

I raised the glass to my lips and saw one of the prunes which gave the liqueur its title rise out of the mire to meet me. When it was harvested in the early 60's it must have been a fine specimen of its kind. In its twilight years and covered in a hoary frosting of mould, however, it was a truly pitiful sight. I shot a desperate glance at Fabrice. He pulled a face, as if to say, 'we don't have much choice.' Out of the corner of my eye I saw our hostess set her own glass aside. "Doctors orders," she quacked gaily. "He says I'm not to drink."

The Gnome was already chawing on his prune and making little grunting noises as if he was sampling some rare delicacy. I glanced under the table in the hope of discovering a dumb mutt, a starving cat, or even a rabid hamster if it would eat that rotted prune. Nothing doing. Bravely I lifted the glass to my lips and nearly gagged as they were met by white flakes of mould which broke surface and formed a fine, white pellicle like ash after a volcanic eruption. I shuddered, then sucked up the rotted fruit between my lips and let it slip down, pip-and- all, like a giant glob of oyster. Mother rummaged in her tin and handed us a clawful of biscuits. I seized them gratefully - anything to take away the impression I'd just swallowed a dead man's kidney - but the aged goodies clung to my palate like clay to a spade.

Meanwhile Mother was evidently having the time of her life. "Eat - after all, you never know what's going to eat us!" she chortled encouragingly. "Is it good?" she asked Fabrice.

He patted his stomach and rolled his eyes. "Delightful," he said.

Satisfied she turned to me. "Good?" she enquired.

"Absolutely delicious," I lied.

She eyed me suspiciously. "*Quoi?*" She said.

Was she deaf, as well as blind? "*Tray bonn,*" I bellowed, waving my glass in the air and praying she wouldn't offer me a refill.

Her eyes rolled round the room as if she was seeking an intruder. "I think she's confused by your accent," Fabrice explained to me in English. "She is an *Anglaise,*" he said to Mother in French.

"*Anglaise?*" Mother repeated as if he'd said 'Martian'.

"It is the best *liqueur de prune que j'ai jamais* tasted," I said hypocritically.

Mother turned on Fabrice in fury. "We aren't in *Angleterre* now - tell her to speak *Français* for the name of God!"

"But *je suis* speaking *Français*," I squeaked indignantly.

Mother rounded on me furiously. *"Q-U-O-I?"* she bawled and the plates rattled on her French dresser.

Patiently Fabrice translated my French into French, but by this time Mother had given up. "Les *Anglais,* huh! What more can you expect from the ones who killed our Joan of Arc?" she sneered.

In the long silence which followed this temporary breakdown in diplomatic relations a fly, brought to life by the stifling heat in the kitchen, bashed madly at the window pane and the Gnome, who was snug in his corner by the fire once more, snored peacefully, totally oblivious of a fat, orange cat which had turned his bald, white head into a comfortable pillow.

"There's a lot of 'your lot' out there," mother said eventually. She waved scornfully towards the window. "Buying up old ruins - paying good money for bad rubbish - *pah*," she spat. There was another pause, but it was ruminative this time - I could tell by her dentures which clicked in time with her brooding thoughts like enamel castanets.

"Still. I suppose if folks have nothing better to do with their money,." she finally said and her tone was strangely mollified. She fixed me as if she was a snake-charmer and I was the silly reptile who was about to make her fortune. "Of course, if there are those who really want to buy , it becomes easier to understand the charm of a *really good* ruin," she added and her voice was oozing comprehension now. She hobbled over to the window and flung back the creaking shutters. " At the right price I might be persuaded to part with one of mine," she said. Together we surveyed the devastated village. "What about this one?" she suggested and she pointed to a three-walled hovel which she seemed to find particularly *'des-res'*.

"Looks like it did battle with a bulldozer and the bulldozer won," sniggered Fabrice.

"Just needs a slap of plaster and a dash of paint", said Mother defensively. "You can see it has loads of potential. It just needs a little love," she added. It was quite uncanny the way she'd instinctively adopted the Estate Agent spiel. She reminded me of an extremely wily broker who once tried to sell me 'a bread oven with a view'.

She took my arm in a pincer grip and manoeuvred me over to the window. "Lovely situation," she enthused, pointing to a wreck which wouldn't have looked out of place in war-torn Kosovo. "South-facing and.." she scanned the huddle of stones desperately seeking some other selling point. "..and gets plenty of light," she ended lamely.

"Which is hardly surprising seeing it hasn't got a roof or walls," quipped Fabrice.

Mother ignored him. "Just needs a little work doing," she said. She was almost pleading with me now. I could feel her willing me to produce fistfuls of cash and confirm - what she'd always secretly thought - that if she could just unearth the right (English) pigeon it would turn out she was sitting on a little goldmine. I left Fabrice to explain that I was not in the least bit interested in her ruins. "Of course not!" She huffed slamming the shutters shut. "And who in their right mind would be?" She stared around her at the immense oak beams, antique furniture and imposing granite fireplace in her own house then she spat as if they'd done her a personal injury. "Old rubbish," I heard her mutter. "Who in their right mind would want any of it, when they could have a brand new bungalow for the same price?"

The Gnome gave a loud snort and sat up. "Mother dreams of a house in town, near the shops and the doctor and the cemetery," he said sleepily.

Mother's eyes glazed over and for long seconds she was lost in contemplating impossibly gleaming vistas of pink Lino and lime Formica. "Who else but you English?" she concluded with a disgusted snort.

I decided it was time I took a stand. Via my interpreter I suggested it was good for everyone if the English bought up ruins that no-one else wanted and stopped villages from dying off.

"Yes, but what do they want to come here for? There's nothing to do out here. What do they come here for – you tell me that?" Mother said plaintively.

"For the fresh air, the beautiful scenery and the unspoilt countryside," I had Fabrice 'translate'.

"Fresh air and unspoilt countryside?" The look she gave me plainly said I should be locked up. "What do they really come here for, hey? I've heard it said they come here because they're criminals and they come to do their nasty business because its isolated - that's what the butcher says. He says that's why their houses are shut up half the time. It's because they just come here to do their crimes. Why else would they want to settle in such a Godforsaken hole?" She dismissed me with disgust and turned to Fabrice. "Do you know the English who's bought a house near Surau?" She asked him. He shook his head. "Bah, it's the usual old ruin - you know the sort they like: all dark and damp and down by a river full of snakes and rats. Anyway, this English, just like the rest of them, only comes to his house once a year. Since he's never there the farmer next door thought it was normal to go on piling his manure up against the rear wall of the English's house – just like he's always done. But that wasn't good enough for the English. He had to go and complain. He said that Nini's good manure was a nuisance and brought smells into his house and flies." She grimaced, as if to say 'milk sop'. "So the English invited Nini the farmer and Claude, our Mayor, round to his house for drinks and after a few bottles of the English's best whisky Claude and Nini swore they'd do something about the manure." She broke off and started to cackle.

"Well that's good, isn't it?" said Fabrice.

"Good?" she gasped. "I'll say it was good. I haven't had such a laugh in years." She blew her nose loudly. "You see, when the English came back a few months later, there was no more manure against his wall," she said and started to cackle even louder.

Fabrice and I stared at each other, mystified. She was wheezing so hard that tears ran down her cactus-wrinkled cheeks.. "Well, surely that was good?" Fabrice enquired again.

"Oh, it was. It was!" she cackled, clutching her sides. "You see the bulldozer from the commune had come and dug a trench two meters wide to carry it away – oh, I never thought the old Mayor had it in him. He's got my vote at the next elections for sure."

"So what is wrong with this trench?" said Fabrice a trifle impatiently.

"Nothing wrong with it at all, " she guffawed. "Except I don't think it's what the English expected. You see the trench cuts right past the front of his house and empties Nini's manure out into the river in the bottom of his garden."

CHAPTER SIX

After weeks of bucketing rain the sky was the smeary blue of a half-washed window pane and the sun drew steam from the pitted roads. It was mid October and leaves were turning brown on the trees and piles of apples lay rotting beneath them in the tangled grass.

"It's my wife, you see - *elle ne fournit plus,*" said père Renard and I'd been chatting with our next-door neighbour for several minutes before he'd come out with this mystifying statement. Just seconds before we'd been exchanging views on cattle farming and his bushy brows had caterpillared up and down as I'd described the antics of veal protestors across the channel. "*Les* English are..," he began and then he'd coughed and after casting a surreptitious glance at me corrected himself with: "..the world is crazy." After which had ensued a brief verbal tussle with world madness in which he, *père* Renard, emerged as the sole hope for sanity on the planet, and then he'd gone off at a tangent about his wife.

'*Fournir*,' I pondered now. I knew that the verb was generally associated with the electricity board, or a dairy herd, and generally meant 'to provide'. Now I knew that milk cows were said to no longer 'provide' – and the electricity board was notorious for 'providing' at an exorbitant price - but his wife?

At that point Renard's brief - yet eloquent - gesture towards the flies of his sagging corduroys enlightened me. "It is the age you see – she no longer wants it," he said sadly and not even the sight of Fabrice emerging from the house clad in thigh-length waders and a beekeepers mask could bring a smile to his sex-starved lips.

Fabrice was dressed to do battle with his worst enemy. We'd woken up that morning to find the corridor awash with toilet waste. "*La merde* is like that," said Renard, who was watching Fabrice now with gloomy interest. "Just when you think its gone forever, it comes backing up on your own door step," he said and his sepulchral tones seemed to imply that Watergate was nothing compared to the treachery of raw sewage.

We watched as Fabrice got his spade out started digging. After a few minutes there was a loud 'clunk' which said he'd found the lid of the septic tank. The promise of a ringside seat at this cesspit romp seemed to have opened up hitherto unexplored recesses of Renard's mind and after snorking over the garden fence a few times he reverted to our earlier conversation and admitted ruefully: "Of course I'm not what I used to be either. I used to climb up on her at least once a month, but these days.." he broke off and shook his head sadly, then turned to watch the action again.

Fabrice was working away at the moss-furred tank with a crowbar now. "Can't ever have been opened – it's jammed solid," he yelled and then there was a juddering thud, the lid slid aside and after teetering on the brink as if bound by some scatological spell, with an audible grunt of fear Fabrice toppled in headlong.

"Garn - get in there!" bawled Renard rubbing his hands in glee. Fabrice came up gasping and Renard was overjoyed at this opportunity to make a witty play on words. "Now you're really in the *'merde'*," he cackled.

I contemplated the love of my life - the man who'd wooed me in Chanel blazers and used to work at the Palace of Versailles - wallowing like a Hippo in unmentionable brown slime and it struck me that only I, who knew of the unspeakable horror of his childhood and the septic tank, could truly appreciate what a nightmare this must be for him.

Fabrice scrabbled gasping and spitting at the ledge of the narrow tank, desperately trying to get a foothold but the ancient excrement was as smooth as axle grease and he slid heavily back into the pit.

"Don't mess around - unblock it whilst you're down there," bellowed Renard. "And don't forget to bring some out for my garden, either," he added as Fabrice came up coughing and spitting for a third time. Renard turned away in disgust. "Townies!" he snorted, neatly forgetting that he'd been a 'townie' himself before he'd retired from Parisian life some 20 years ago. "Now if I was a little younger..," he added and the ensuing pause was fertile with significance. If Renard were a little younger I was to understand that he would have been in that tank like a ferret up a trouser leg - nothing on earth would have given him more pleasure than to spend a sunny afternoon up to his armpits in our offal. In fact, I was given to comprehend, it would have been a positive joy for Renard to battle with our wayward alluvium, if only he'd been a few years younger. But as it was, alas! He sighed once, or twice and shook his head and having neatly shrugged off the burden of a guilty conscience, settled back to enjoy the rest of the show.

Just then there was a muffled cry of triumph and Fabrice staggered out of the pit brandishing a plunger, festooned with dank loops of pink paper, victoriously. "I think I've unblocked the tank," he said advancing on me. "Give us a kiss?" he added with a leer.

I backed off hastily and collided with Renard who seized this heaven-sent opportunity to grope my buttocks. From the nether regions I heard a strangled sob. *"Ma femme ne fournit plus,"* came his aching cry and he staggered blindly off down the path.

On a chilly morning a few weeks later, as we waited in a huddle by the roadside for the butchers van to appear, there was a loud squawking overhead and we looked up to see an arrow-shaped cloud of pterodactyls flying high in the misted sky. Granny told us these were grey herons and they were winging their way to warmer climes. I shivered and wished I could wing-it with them.

"They're early. That means it's going to be a cold winter," she told us.

Already her sayings studded our lives – just as they'd long ago transformed her own existence into a minefield of 'do's and 'don'ts'. Time, after time she advised us not to do the washing up if the cat coughed, as we would surely catch pleurisy - luckily

Typhus had turned half wild since moving to the countryside, so the risk was slight. Cutting hair in March was another 'no, no', because this merry month was propitious for migraines, it seemed. She also advised us to avoid crossroads, as this was where the Devil lay in wait, and with the festive season drawing nigh she solemnly warned us against entering a stable at any time around Christmas eve. "The animals kneel down and pray then and since it's a bit embarrassing for them - being animals and all - they take their holy precautions and if you do enter and see them, you'll die an 'orrible death before the year's out," she informed us with evident relish.

Extra complications were added to Granny's life by the postman's calendar. This Wiseman's almanac, which she bought from one of the postie's factotum's each year, awarded every day to a different saint, and since each saint had his, or her 'specialty' - St Catherine's was the day to plant shrubs, St Simon's was ideal for making pâté, etc - juggling with this pot-pourri of local sayings and holy wisdom, took up a great deal of her time. Especially now, when the most important day of the year was fast approaching. This was *Le Toussaint*, the 1st of November, the day when all the saints in her calendar were brought together, along with the population of France's cemeteries, for a massive festival of death.

'It's an ill wind that blows no good', they say, and this deathly day must have made Mr Khrusos Anthemon a very happy man. Whether it was fussy poodle pom-poms, blousy blond baseballs, or avant-garde green spikes, in shop stands and on market stalls Chrysanthemums were bursting out all over and that unmistakable dry-rot odour, with its aura of pithead misery and mining misfortune so dear to D.H. Lawrence, filled the autumn air like melancholic fog.

Fabrice's mother and his depressed sister from Paris were the family's cemetery reps that year and they arrived at Mouzon on the 31st October, late at night. The following morning we were summoned at the crack of sunrise and after a lukewarm coffee in the weak dawning light, our morbid day began.

It's hardly surprising there are so many accidents on French roads on November 1st: with so many pots of chrysanthemums stacked up on passenger seats, overflowing from boots, or tied to roofs and bonnets drivers can hardly see a thing. Fabrice's mad mother was no exception. Never the best of drivers at the best of times, for the sake of family honour she'd bought up the stock of half the florist shops in Paris and had somehow managed to cram her grim booty into the body of her battered Renault *Cinq*. As we drove at hair-raising speed down the narrow country roads with three plants nestling on the brake pedal, a mass of pink puffballs in her lap and a huge plant looming from behind her in the backseat and twining it's leaves round her neck, she twitched violently and brushed away a flower, or coughed spasmodically as she spat out several leaves. Imperturbable as death itself in the passenger seat beside her, Fabrice's Depressed Sister stared out at the horrors of rural life from behind a screen of waving, pink petals.

Under louring skies and over lumbering roads, we joined the world-and-his-wife for a crazed treasure hunt, with a grave theme. Our mission was to manage a trip out to the most distant tombs, of the most distant relatives, before the day ended, or before the flowers ran out, whichever came first. At 9am on-the-dot, we pulled up at our first destination: the cemetery in Massignac. Parting her mini-jungle Fabrice's mother peered short-sightedly into the rear-view mirror, pursued her mouth coquettishly and carefully applied several coats of rouge to her ageing lips. In order to properly honour the gruesome day she'd left the scandalously young boyfriend behind her in Paris and was clad in an unusually sober, black, tailored costume. But she hadn't been able to resist painting her nails bright mauve and when she staggered out of the car carrying her chrysanthemums I saw that respect for the Grim

Reaper hadn't prevented her donning scarlet, fishnet stockings either.

In contrast to visitor's sober habits, the cemetery was gay with colour. Flowers were as bright as Smarties and kids clad in their Sunday-best, played hide-and-seek and giggled as they jumped on the bones of their long dead ancestors. At the graveside of a toothy cousin who'd been photographed in a virgin's robe for posterity, and then been ravished post-haste by consumption, Fabrice's barmy parent produced a bucket and a brush, tugged pink plastic gloves over her varnished puce nails and set to work vigorously scrubbing virescent mould from the tomb, under the cousin's watchful eye.

At another resting place she whipped out a screwdriver and with surprising dexterity for a woman who believed women were merely ornamental, removed a copper plaque and popped it in her panther-skin handbag, to be taken home and lovingly refurbished by a top-class undertaker in the rue St Honoré.

By teatime I was heartily sick of cemeteries. The best plants had been distributed according to the family's rating system and we were down to 5cm pots, or a few blousy cuttings which we stuck into the damp earth around each grave. Suddenly the Depressed Sister, who'd trailed round behind us most of the time picking at her spots, or pinching the arms of kids who dared to err too close, pointed to a middle-of-the-range plant which neatly expressed the ambivalent sentiments of it's donor and let out a shriek. "I don't recognise that Chrysanthemum, mum!" she cried.

'Mum' swung round and glared at the offending plant. In Toussaint terms, this was 'an incident'.

After examining the offending floral arrangement like it was a body on the slab at the morgue, Fabrice's mother concluded it came from *tante* Hélène and if the Stygian ferry had hoved-to and offered her a lift, she would not have looked more thunderstruck. From her foaming lips we learnt that *tante* Hélène had been disinherited by her own mother in favour of a scheming niece and then cast off by the rest of her family when she caused a scandal over her mother's fresh-dug grave. Fifteen years tides had washed over fifteen years sands since that fateful day, but for Fabrice's nutty mother we were talking 'yesterday' and the trip back home was one, long imprecation.

That night over dinner, as she swilled the cognac-based beverage called 'Pineau' and spat excited pellets of baguette out over the table and waved her arms around like a drowning octopus, Fabrice's peculiar parent introduced me to all the other skeletons which had rattled around in the family's cupboard for the past few decades. There was aunt Gaby, an ageing prostitute who had been shunned by the family - not because of moral outrage, but because she'd refused to share her ill-gotten gains. There was a great aunt who'd collaborated with the Nazis and was deeply despised because she had nothing to show for it. There was an uncle with one arm, who voted Le Pen and lived in a council flat, there was an ageing brother who'd been written off for good because he was hopelessly gay, there was a sister who'd run away with a gypsy and was no longer respectable and there was a cousin, twice-removed, who'd sold stolen lots of motors and made loads of lovely money, but had been struck off the family's register when he'd been stupid enough to get caught and sent to prison. And as the alcohol began to course through her veins Fabrice's dotty parent started to reminisce about her own father. "P..poor P..papa was gassed out during the first World War. He just wasn't the same with only one lung," she sputtered. "M..mother - *hic!* - always said it was that - *hic!* - missing lung which turned him into an alca..alca - *hic!* - holic."

Later that evening she dragged us all to mass in Mouzon's massive, mediaeval church and as I watched candlelight flicker over the aged stone walls and twinkle on the Virgin's well-varnished robes, I reflected that another reason for all the road accidents at *le Toussaint* was because - whether it was to get maudlin and remember, or get merry and forget - entire families got blind, steaming drunk. According to statistics it was the French public holiday which had the most mortal road accidents. Musing on this, as the priest warned against the sins of the flesh and Fabrice's half-crazed mother jiggered up and down beside me trying to stifle her drunken hiccups, like a cricket with it's hind legs stuck in superglue, an odd, irreverent thought popped into my head. Wasn't it rather ironic to think it was on the very day of the year when French cemeteries were most visited, that the Grim Reaper who watched over them, made his biggest cull?

No more sitting outside on the splintered bench under the shade of the lichen-barked cherry tree. No more supping on fresh goats cheese from the local farm served with Granny's home-grown tomatoes splitting their sides with flavour. Winter had come and stripped the tree of shade. It had covered the bench with a thick sheet of ice and it's needles had punctured the last of Granny's tomatoes. Even her vegetable plot lay dormant, now. A few cabbages stuck green heads out from the top of an icy blanket, a few carrots poked red toes out at the bottom - and a frill of lettuces round the midriff managed to soldier on with the aid of a cold frame - but the ready money of fresh vegetables had grown scarce and it was a vital currency for Granny. When the boredom of village life threatened to drive her up the wall it allowed her to come knocking on ours, and other people's, doors with offerings of string beans and corn salad. After all, exchanging vegetables that she had too much of, anyway, was a small price to pay for an afternoon's guaranteed gossiping.

But now even Granny was forced to stay inside and the road outside our house was deserted. Not even Dédé could be heard chundering about on his moped. It was freezing cold. Even the cow pats had iced so hard that driving over them in our old Deux CV was like driving over wooden springs. Instead of standing outside and chatting, neighbours poked their noses out of doors, sniffed the air, shook their heads and hurried back inside to the comfort of hot food, Benny Hill and a wood burning stove. We realised that Granny and her herons were right: winter looked set to be mercilessly cold.

Most evenings as hibernal cold nibbled slow, but sure, at the fast-shrinking nub of day, we'd go and fetch the milk. "Here come the tourists!" the farmer inevitably exclaimed - he was not alone in thinking we couldn't possibly be here to stay. We'd been at Mouzon several months, but we were still pointed out and discussed wherever we went. It wasn't yet fashionable to move to the countryside - and there weren't many people our age who'd choose to live in such tiny, out of the way village. Add to that the fact that I was English – which was nearly unheard of at the time and in this area - and Fabrice was from Paris, which was the moon as far as most local folk were concerned, you understood why, like it, or not – and even though Fabrice's family had a house in the village - we were 'the outsiders'.

"You should worry," grumbled Pere Renard when I mentioned this. "I've lived here for twenty years and they still call me 'the Parisian'."

So we played the role assigned to us, and trotted out, like tourists, into the freezing, starlit nights to fetch our pails of milk – and just like tourists we gloried in the quaintness of it all. In the long, low barns behind their wooden byres the buff cows mooed plaintively as the farmer and his wife scolded them and spanked their flanks, pushing them aside to leave place for forty more to be milked before supper. To comfort themselves the cows munched hay, sounding like they had crisp mouthfuls of Iceberg lettuce, whilst the milk drilled out beneath them, steaming into the waiting zinc bucket. The air was filled with breast-feeding baby odours creamed across new-mown hay and seemed to concentrate a thousand memories of heat-struck pastures. Sounds had that far-away, fuzzy-edged feel like when you listen through a shell, or through the echo at the local swimming pool and it was a quality which perfectly suited the yester-year atmosphere.. Through cracks in the tiled barn roof the moon set a sensual, silver glint to the hard yellow straw and in the dim light the cows were as big as hairy mammoths and the milking farmer and his wife sat on stools beneath them, were like five-legged insects clinging to their giant flanks.

Come hail or ice, we wouldn't have missed our self-imposed milk duty for the world. For us it had the mythical charm of a nativity scene and we felt eminently romantic emerging from the barn with our hot pails of milk, which we used as finger warmers for the long walk home. "How lucky these people are to live in the countryside, living far from all the noise and stress of the city, and waking up everyday in this country paradise," we told each other. But we were hopelessly prejudiced. We *wanted* everything to be perfect, so we projected only the magical image we wanted to see. We refused to perceive the other side of the rural picture: the struggle to survive, the monotony of people's lives and the grinding boredom which turned the slightest thing into an event.

Our one-sided judgements extended to winter also. Whatever Granny had said I was convinced that this was 'the south' and therefore winters should be mild. It took -5 celcius on the thermometer for five days running to shatter that particularly tenacious illusion. On the fifth of these memorable mornings for the first time in our pampered lives Fabrice and I started to take an unhealthy interest in thermal underwear.

When we awoke on the fifth day there was thick frost on the inside of the bedroom window and a howling draught which turned steaming coffee to instant ice. We finally managed to struggle out of the cosy bed and piled on every other item of clothing we could find (in Fabrice's case this included several pairs of his grandpa's woolly leggings and a knitted bonnet like the ones you find on top of hard-boiled eggs) and clad like this we hurried to the local store as soon as it was light, to buy thermal vests and long-johns.

In the nearby town of Chasseneuil Christmas was everywhere. Branches of pine decked out in fussy bows and gleaming baubles, decorated every street corner. Plastic Santas had crawled into a dozen chimneys and were hiking up a dozen shop fronts, and decorated lights and tinned music had transformed the main thoroughfare into a mini Oxford Circus.

80

Here in the countryside a visit to the shops, especially at the festive season, was considered to be 'an event' and it was de rigueur to dress up. Even women who wore the most tattered housecoats during the week would deck themselves out in clean pinafores for the weekly shopping chore. As for their farmer-husbands they tottered, noticeably uncomfortable, over knife-edge creases in their brand new, navy blue trousers. Which is why our appearance in the local supermarket, clad in every item of clothing we possessed plus a splatter of mud for good measure, caused a minor stir. Only gypsies and beggars, dressed like this. Behind us in the queue a young woman sniffed the air and then stared at us in horror. Totally oblivious, Fabrice filched the free chocolates which were left by the till in a saucer during the festive season and munched them appreciatively. Having watched us through the shop to make sure we didn't steal anything, when we reached the checkout the cashier had pity in her eyes. As we drew level with her she gave us a knowing wink. "If you go over there you can get some new clothes," she bellowed pointing at a grimy shop window opposite.

Everyone in the queue stared at me as I stared at her finger, mystified. "Is it a shop?" I asked. I heard someone giggle.

"Oh don't worry you don't have to pay. It's a charity shop and for people like you everything's free," the cashier brayed.

Day after day the pitiless cold continued and we surged around the old, cold house like Tweedledum and Tweedledee. Each night we removed a few layers and slid into bed and each morning we piled them all back on again and slid, shivering, into the icy morning air. For the first time in my life I could sympathise with the problems of amorous porcupines: with all these layers between the two of us each night, the most we could do in bed was rub noses.

We were down to the last few logs and our last square metre of wood and still the temperatures plummeted. At - 8 Celsius the taps froze solid, the toilet froze over and our feet went dead. Handling forks with gloved fingers was becoming second nature and Fabrice, who suffered badly from the cold, had taken the veil. It was a flowery one belonging to his batty mother and he used it to cover his face up entirely, only lifting a flap to facilitate the passage of vital things, like food.

At -10 Celsius it got too cold to bear, so we sat out in the car with the motor running until we could no longer afford the petrol. After that we bustled around a lot or, when icicles started to form, hugged the cat who had never received so much affection in his life. For the first time in our lives we were experiencing what it was to be really cold. For the first time in our lives we were also learning what it was like to be really poor.

Necessities, such as wood for the stove and thermal underwear, had rapidly swallowed up our meagre savings and after that each meal was a challenge to ingenuity. Gathering dandelion leaves from the fields we made salads. Fallen apples left to rot at roadsides became cheap purées for inexistent roasts - and sweet pies on the days when we could afford to buy sugar. We discovered the value of canned tomatoes – only 0,25 centimes a tin! – and they became the base for everything we ate. With flour and a bit of milk they made tomato soup. A few crumbly potatoes added, added up to tomato stew. An old crust of cheese and a few crusts of bread thrown in and - hey presto! - we had a tomato gratin. Even the cat, faced with that or starvation, had learnt to like tinned tomatoes. It was uncomfortable alright, but - for the moment at least - our discomfort had a novelty appeal. We'd always been able to buy whatever we wanted. We came from over-heated flats with overflowing freezers and we'd grown as soft as overripe tomatoes ourselves from scoffing all that easy food. Now every mouthful counted and - far from being miserable all the time - to our surprise we derived a certain pleasure in redefining what we'd always considered essential; in learning to do without.

Lack of the basics was one thing, however. Christmas without a tree was quite another. They cost 20 francs at the local store which was out of the question on our meagre budget. With the aid of Granny's calendar we chose a moonless night and with temperatures plummeting to around - 15 Celsius we set out for the vast pine forests of Sauvagnac.

Clusters of icy stars struck flinty sparks off the low, sweeping boughs as we swished along the sandy track. An owl flew out, stared a moment with fanatical eyes into our the headlights, then veered into the forest opposite. I'd taught Fabrice a Christmas carol and he hummed it now. "Oh leetle town of Bet-le-em ow still we see zee lie," he warbled and when he got to the verse about 'deep and dreamless sleep' it was as if he was singing this forest's enchantment.. A few yards further down the track Fabrice pulled over to the side as a sleepy Robin, puffed up with cold like a tennis ball, bounced out into our path. The car door creaked open and we were bathed in a heavenly fragrance which made me think of lemon skins burning over a sweet, wood fire. Slender points of ice hung from the pine branches like stalagmites, or cracked and fell with a 'Jingle Bell's' tinkle on the car's canvas roof. The forest floor was still matted with needles from the previous year and cones lay half-buried, marked by the teeth of hungry squirrels, like partly exploded grenades.

Fabrice pulled out a rusted saw and stuffed it under his coat, then we set out to find 'our tree'. Above us the night sky was naked now. It had thrust off all trace of cloud cover and seemed to be concentrating it's energy on freezing the earth's crust. "Cold, cold, cold," our teeth chattered in sympathy. For once I was thankful for Fabrice's sempiternal boiled-egg hat - getting lost in the forest on such a cold night would have meant instant hypothermia, but his jangling pom-pom guided me through the gloom like a kitsch, knitted version of the traditional Shepherd's star.

Ignoring the arctic conditions Fabrice was rigorously fussy, passing candidates over with bitter grunts.. "Not enough branches," I heard him mutter or: "'this peak just isn't long enough."

Making our way past high tree stumps and low branches, we bashed along blindly for nearly an hour until he discovered what he considered to be *le* perfect tree. It had a welter of branches which fanned out in a perfect pyramid and the peak snaked up to well-above head height and – I thought it was a trick of the light – the branches shone pale blue.

Fabrice whipped out his saw. "Be better using my teeth," I heard him mutter and for a minute I thought he was and then I realised that odd gnawing sound was a car heading down the icy track. Just time to admire the pines picked out in the headlights like sugar cut-outs, before we were rolling over and over into the thorny undergrowth. Later, as we loaded up the tree and screeched off down the track and I'd picked most of the bramble thorns out of my punctured backside, I nagged Fabrice angrily. "I don't see why you panicked like that. They can't hang us for taking one, measly tree," I moaned.

Wrapped up in a boar-hair jacket and wearing a stylish fox-fur scarf with spotted black and white rabbit-skin gloves to match, *Père* Buissard was hovering outside when we arrived back in Mouzon and unloaded our spoils. "That's a beauty. Where did you get it?" he asked.

"On the m..market," I stammered

He frowned suspiciously. "You got a Douglas Blue on the market?" He shook his head. "Ony if I were you I wouldn't try taking them from the forest - them wardens have got orders to shoot on sight," he said

CHAPTER SEVEN

Fabrice dumped a scratching, clawing bundle wrapped in a flurry of red tinsel, on the bed. "Merry Christmas," he cried and an ornamental Typhus let out a yowl and fled.

It was still freezing cold outside, but brilliant sunlight was slowly melting ice on the window pane. Fabrice set a breakfast tray in front of me. "Last of the bread, last of the butter, last of the jam and a third reheat of the last of the coffee," he enumerated. Then he crawled back into bed and there was a strange glint in his eye. He was holding a letter.. It was from his father. He opened it triumphantly and waggled a 200 hundred France note.

"Two *stères* of cheap firewood," I muttered mechanically.

"Two bottles of gas for the cooker," he said.

I thought of Typhus. "75 cheap tins of cat food," I added.

"A couple of roast chickens?" he said tentatively.

"A bloody mountain of tinned tomatoes," I said flatly.

That clinched it. He leapt out of bed. "I'll just go and make the phone call, then," he said.

Neither of us had the slightest intention of being sensible. If we'd thought life was about pension plans and fructifying nest eggs we'd probably never have left the city at all. If we were perfectly prepared to make a virtue of necessity when absolutely necessary, we certainly weren't averse to making hay when the sun shone either – and the sun was shining now in the shape of a 200 franc bill. We both knew that *manyana* would be an *otras dias*, but, for this day at least we were going to throw caution to the wind and have a ball. It was our first Christmas in the Charente countryside and we were going to celebrate in style.

We'd slathered over the special Christmas menus, which seemed to have been printed in the local newspapers just to taunt us, for weeks so we were perfectly prepared. Like broken-down jockeys with alcohol-misted plans of returning to the saddle 'one day', we'd constantly studied the form. We knew that this one boasted 'as much wine as you can drink', that that one offered what it described enticingly as, 'an endless buffet'. We'd seen restaurants proposing a full set menu and free champagne, others which dangled goodies like hot foie gras baked in caramel' and 'duck stuffed with truffles' to tempt us and impossible dreams of such fabulous joys had kept us going on our monotonous diet of tomatoes *à toutes les sauces*. But in terms of sheer, unbelievable value for money the chateau restaurant of Torsac was several hurdles ahead of the rest of the restaurateurs in the running.

At Torsac the Chef proposed a champagne *Kir*, two *entrées*, including the Christmas-ubiquitous foie gras, a main course served with all the trimmings, plus cheese, salad, wine and coffee for the ridiculous price of 100 francs per head.

Fabrice returned from the frozen phone box. He was grinning from ear to ear. "I've booked," he said, "and for that price you aren't taking a risk. Even if the fine chateau-restaurant turns out to be a stinking mediaeval fleapit, in quantity at least we're sure to eat like kings."

"And one thing's for sure - we won't feel out of place," I added and with these words hovering in the air we went upstairs to dress - only to discover that the eternal question "what shall I wear?" takes on an entirely new meaning when you dwell at the heart of a green-wood bonfire in sub-zero temperatures.

After much huffing and blowing Fabrice appeared in the bedroom doorway. "How do I look?" he asked coyly.

He struggled to sound casual, but I could tell he was hanging on my reply. Desperately I tried to wipe the smirk from my face.

He was wearing the smart trousers of his only remaining dress-suit, but they strained as tight as a distended balloon over three pairs of thermal long-johns. On the top half I could just make out a dinner jacket - it peeped out from beneath two woolly sweaters which had grown octopus arms in the last wash and were rolled back in slack, cellulite folds, along his upper arms. With his handsome - if weather-worn - features, the boiled-egg bonnet clamped firmly to his head and clad in such a pick-and-mix accoutrement, he looked like a degenerate playboy who'd lost his entire fortune at the gambling table, then been down and out in Paris - several times.

I struggled to find something to say. "For someone who sleeps in a cardboard box you'd look absolutely fine," I finally said.

He smirked at what he considered to be a back-handed compliment. "It's a Versace suit, you know," he said with a hint of pride. He gave a twirl and the sweater's floppy sleeves unravelled and swung out around him like umbrella spokes. When he came to a halt once more they dangled down to well below his knees.

"I'm sure Mr Versace would be very proud," I said and we headed for the car.

Blue-rinsed hair encased in a purple hairnet and feet shod in elegant beaver-hair slippers, Madame Renard was drawing water from her well. She nearly dived over the edge with her bucket at the sight of Fabrice's puffy-yet-elegant attire. "Fancy Dress?" she suggested tentatively.

Père Renard who'd come out to see the fun, snorted disdainfully at his wife's lack of *savoir vivre*. "It is the latest fashion. It is how all the youngsters dress nowadays. It is 'le grunge'," he scolded her and then he fixed me with a long, lingering stare.

It must be said I was quite a picture. With my blonde hair carefully combed back in a bob, a thick, woollen shawl wrapped round my head, two pairs of fishermen's woollen socks in high-heeled, velvet shoes and a paint-stained army Mac over my slinky black dress, he obviously found me highly desirable. "That," he instructed his wife, " is the very latest in chic."

.

The Auberge of the Chateau of Torsac stood on a slope dominating the village to which it gave it's name. Several 15th century towers carved crenulated edges out of the frosty air and far beneath the river trailed a sluggish load of water, thickened to white sauce by the cold. On the long drive to the tiny village in the warm car we shed layer after layer of clothing and by the time we arrived our battered old Duck looked like the scene of a striptease organised in aid of Oxfam.

The waitress greeted us at the entrance. We stared around us wildly. "Are you sure there is no mistake - the menu really is..?" Fabrice burbled.

"..Hundred francs," she snapped and she led us to a table, which was impeccably decked with a red and green linen cloth and laid up with silverware and crystal, right in the middle of a magnificent, high-vaulted hall. I hobbled after her, vainly attempting to rub dollops of mud off my high heeled shoes. Laying the menu in front of us she vanished. We stared around us slightly overawed, at the oak tables, ornate chairs, immense chandeliers and floor covered with ancient, pitted flagstones. A dozen festively-decked tables floated alongside us. They were all empty. It was like being in a French chateau version of the Marie Celeste. "Where's everyone else?" asked Fabrice when the waitress bustled back into the room once more.

She shrugged. "It is the economic *crise*. No-one has any money," she said and she plugged a fan heater into the wall, shoved it under the table at our feet and vanished once more.

In all decency we knew this was the moment when we should have muttered something like: "Goodness - we can't possibly let her go to all this trouble just for us!" and politely taken our leave. But neither of us had the slightest intention of 'doing the decent thing'. After months of abstemious living this unabashed hedonism – the luxury of having a castle, a waitress, a chef and an entire kitchen staff all at our disposal – was far too good to be missed. So we sat back and prepared to enjoy it to the full.

As we clinked glasses of bubbling champagne *Kir* and congratulated each other, the kitchen door swung open with a squeeze box wail and out popped the waitress again. Behind her we caught a glimpse of heat-steamed faces floating in an exotic mist, which bellied out around the restaurant like a gastronomic ectoplasm teasing us with cordon bleu come-hither aromas. The entire kitchen was a hell-house of activity: pans were popping, stoves were raging, pots were stewing and cauldrons bubbling - and all for our unique pleasure!

A glass of sticky-sweet Pineau arrived and then foie gras piping hot, served on brown bread toast. Fabrice obligingly explained how the *'foie'* was made and went into great detail about how the geese were funnel-fed. I tasted it anyway. It rubbed like raw silk over my tongue and had a subtle, nutty aftertaste. "Delicious - I'll never eat it again," I said.

The door wheezed open once more and along with an odorous fog, the waitress squeezed out almost completely hidden by a kind-of seafood leaning Pisa. She staggered the lengthy route to our table and the tall wire basket of oysters, crushed ice and algae rocked like a ship in high seas.

"*Fine de Claire.* Probably from the island of Oléron," said Fabrice. Like most Frenchman he got deadly serious when it came to the subject of food. Relieved of her burden the waitress skipped lightly back to the kitchen. The door squeezed open and I caught a glimpse of the Chef. He was slumped over the stove, white hat askew, twirling a sauce with gusto as he guzzled from a bottle of red wine. I was glad I preferred savoury dishes. - it was by no means certain he'd make it through to dessert.

With passionate pedantry Fabrice explained that the oysters were green, because of a special algae in the water where they were farmed. Already slightly tipsy from the unaccustomed combination of food, warmth and wine I eyed him with renewed respect. He was no longer just the tramp who shared my hovel, he was a connoisseur. He wasn't just the hobo who hobbled into my bed each night, he was a man who knew about the finer things in life.

"A true gourmet eats with his eyes, as well as his stomach," he explained, as he shovelled up oysters with the speed and technique of a seafood hoover.

I watched respectfully and decided I'd take his word for it. How could I explain to this fervid food fan that the mere sight of oysters made me want to vomit?

Masterful, he insisted I eat one.

I gulped it down, trying to ignore a hybrid texture which reminded me of skinned slugs wrapped in strips of jellyfish and a flavour which was the nearest thing I'd imagine to eating a plate of boiled rubber. Then I shoved two-dozen, minus one, onto his plate and watched as he deftly prepared his favourite delicacy. He slid the rounded oyster knife under the bony shell, then gave a little wriggle and a sharp twist. The oyster popped open. He squirted lemon juice onto the milky, vulnerable-looking jelly in the middle then made a funnel of his lips and putting the shell to them, slurped the oyster down. I watched him curiously. He really did seem to enjoy this disgusting food. I gave up trying to understand and decided it must be like Bird's Nest soup, or Monkey's Brains - that it must be one of those delicacies you had to sup on from the cradle to really understand.

The wine arrived and he did a Gérard Depardieu, thrusting his virile conk into the bell-shaped glass and tilting and sloshing the wine around. Then he gargled it like mouthwash, took a long draught and assured me it was an excellent vintage, with a hint of vanilla and just a *soupçon* of exotic fruits.

I hadn't the heart to tell him I was one of those slobs who finished left-over glasses at parties and could be found, around 3am when all other hope had fled, sniffing in other people's under-stair cupboards in the hope of finding a bottle of their old grand-mamma's Elderberry wine or anything else likely to contain the slightest *soupçon* of alcohol. There are some things it's best not to share and anyway, even I could tell this was good wine - mainly because it didn't set my teeth humming like a dozen galvanized wires when I took a slug.

After the oysters, there was a *'Blanquette de Veau'* served in a thick, creamy sauce, then there was a salad, basted with a spicy mustard dressing and served with a massive wheel of cheeses. After that we ate salty flakes of Roquefort with our fingers and wrapped tangy slivers of goat's cheese in salad and fed them to each other, or sampled slices of Camembert which oozed like lava and stunk like feet and Fabrice said were exactly *'à point'*. After a *'Fondant au chocolat'* which melted in the mouth like vanilla fudge, we had coffee and a digestive and staggered out into the frigid air.

It was the best Christmas meal we ever had. No hand stuck up a half-frozen Turkey, stuffing and squabbling with family members about Trivial Pursuit. No rows about who was to do the washing up, or who did what with poor old Colonel Pepper in the library. It was just a restaurant's entire kitchen staff, the two of us and three, blissful hours of total self-indulgence - and it was wonderful. Little did we know it then, but it was to be our last good feast for a long, long while to come.

CHAPTER EIGHT

The electricity had been cut off two days before and - despite Fabrice's astounding negotiating talents - the water seemed likely to follow. Red letters had come in handy for lighting the fire, until the last log fired all guns and sunk without trace as we'd sat sombrely watching it go up in smoke. We had a gas burner, but no gas to burn it and Shapeless, who had a small store and let us have bottles 'on tick', had developed a nervous tic when we'd asked her for 'just one more'.

For the rest of the morning Fabrice rummaged around the house in the hope of finding something to burn and after sawing the psychedelic sofa in two and giving up on burning it because of poisonous fumes, he sent the collected works of Bernard Buffet up the chimney. Then we had a light tomato lunch and Fabrice went out into the garden and rooted around until he found half a tree. He harnessed me to it like a Husky and bellowed 'heave'. The trunk slid forward, the 'driver' got caught up in his reins and fell flat on his backside and I fell flat on my face in a puddle. Soaked to the skin and freezing cold, it took us two hours to get the tree trunk to our doorstep. Just as we were wondering what to do with the sodden mass, Renard appeared with a chainsaw. He strutted up and down a few times, making it buzz and whine between his thighs as he arboured one of those 'look-what-I've-got-between-my-legs airs generally seen on the faces of ageing pop stars, then he set-to and rapidly mastered our recalcitrant stump.

For the rest of the day we smouldered like hams, wreathed in poisonous green-wood smoke until the last branch burnt and we were once again left wondering what we were going to do. Because we knew that if we didn't find a solution to our heating problem – and soon - we were all set to freeze to death.

It fell in the night. It was the deepest snowfall in Charente for more than half a century and by early morning Mouzon was cut off from the rest of the world. When we woke that morning we knew there was something different. As motes of bright light slid across the bedroom's parquet floor, we realised what it was. There were no cars revving, or butcher's vans honking, or crowing cockerels or villagers gossiping. Outside there was total silence and even the cows seemed to have gone underground. It was like being wrapped inside a velvet cocoon - as if the tiny village was too dumbfounded to try and struggle out of it's inhabitual snowy straitjacket. From the bedroom window I gazed out at the white fur muffling the village up to it's elderly chin. The church was a pale blancmange with a black weathercock stuck on top. The fields seemed to merge with a road that was as smooth as cream and the windblown verges were swept into delicate peaks like several huge lemon meringue pies just waiting to be sent to the oven.

As I watched a door creaked open and Renard emerged, dressed in Sunday best. He stood a moment staring up at the louring sky in disbelief, then he shook his fist. How could the snow have done this to him? Didn't it realize that today wasn't any ordinary Sunday? Didn't it understand that this was the third of the month and the day when OAPs from all over Charente got together for their monthly afternoon tea dance?

He stared mournfully at the snow and spat in disgust. Steam rose from a small, black hole at his slippered feet. How could it be that the weather didn't understand that this was the one day of the month when, he, Renard, got to abandon his wife - 'she who no longer provided' - and play bridge and flirt and shift across a gleaming dance floor with a dozen lovely ladies?'

He stood a long moment, staring sightlessly at the snow, then he rubbed his chin thoughtfully. When he lifted his head there was a new set to his jaw. Even from a distance I could see the French equivalent of 'Dunkirk Spirit' gleaming in his bleary old eyes. A low buzzing filled the air - and I wasn't sure if it was the wind in the wires, or Renard humming '*La Marseillaise*'. With new determination he pulled on rubber wellies and crabbed his way across the ice and snow towards his garage. A few minutes later the garage door rattled open and the pallid, pristine air was poisoned with stinking exhaust fumes. A few moments later still, Renard emerged at the wheel of his lovingly pampered Renault *Cinq*.

Perhaps it's time to point out that, if on foot and around the village Renard was a harmless ambler, behind the wheel he became an evil fiend. He loved his car and spent weekends hoovering the cushions, shining up the bumpers and washing each of it's tyres with the exaggerated care of a love-struck Prince Charming - and if he could have done he probably would've put glass slippers on each of it's dainty little feet as well. When he was inside his little motor, however, Renard was another man. It was as if the sheet of glass, which separated him from the outside world imbued him with mystical powers - as if the sensual touch of fake leather steering wheel, or the sensation of the gearstick's smooth knob transformed an ordinary elderly gent with denture problems into a four-wheeled maniac spawned from Hell. It was hardly surprising that villagers had nicknamed him 'road-rage Renard' and pulled over to the side of the road if they saw him coming.

'Vrum, vruuum,' I heard as one dainty tyre 'stepped' cautiously onto the snowy tarmac. Renard revved some more, gaining much need comfort from his motor's agony - as if each squealing nut, each screeching bolt, was telling him he was in control. Then a second tyre bit on the nasty white stuff and he started to relax. Why, this snow wasn't such a big deal after all. Why, he could almost tell it *merde!* He revved some more and it was easy to see that he'd have liked to wind down a window, rest an elbow on the window ledge and let the four remaining hairs on his shiny pate fly out in the wind like that reckless fellow - what was his name: James Bean? In his minds eye he'd already arrived at the OAP tea dance. He was hailed as a hero: racy Renard the man who'd conquered Mouzon's white wastes. Now he saw a delightful septuagenarian with a daring, bright blue-rinse smiling coyly up at him. "*Voulez vous danser avec moi?*" he heard himself say and he saw her fling herself into his arms, screaming, "*Je veux, je veux!*" His eyes glazed over as he imagined her bony frame rubbing amorously against his own, as they danced and discussed fascinating subjects - such as his lumbago and Maurice the gardener's new remedy for greenfly - whilst 75 year-old André Verchuren and his arthritic orchestra – false teeth and toupees to a man – serenaded the charming couple with yet another slow waltz. He could hear her whisper (in his good ear) that the two of them were 'meant to be' and he could see his *boules* playing pals sidle up to him during the intermission and josh him a shade too heartily, for cradle-snatching.

The scene had shifted now - he was holding the mayor and a shadowy group of local dignitaries, spellbound with tales of his battle through Mouzon's arctic wastes. "Monsieur Renard, I must apologise. You are a hero to this commune and will surely receive a medal - and to think that for all these I have stupidly kept calling you 'The Parisian'," the mayor was saying.

The dream faded abruptly as the car's last wheel bit on icy snow and the vehicle began to slide, slowly, slowly, sideways. The hero of Mouzon panicked. I just caught a glimpse of his eyebrows in the rear-view mirror, semaphoring 'd-i-s-t-r-e-s-s' and then there was a loud plop like a giant egg yolk landing in a floury swimming pool and the car flipped over on it's side in the ditch.

We rushed downstairs. Renard lay full length in the driver's seat moaning loudly. When he saw us he tapped his chest. "It's his heart!" I shrieked

Fabrice snorted loudly. "It's not his heart, it's his wallet. He only bought that car a couple of months ago."

Madame Renard appeared on the doorstep in a blue housecoat with curlers in her hair. Her hands were covered in flour and her reading glasses were slightly askew. She put her head on one side to get the glasses straight and then peered at her husband lying in the upside-down car. The hero of Mouzon's arctic wastes stared up at his other half mournfully. Madame Renard stared down at him and the flaps on her long, pimpled nose started twitching as if she was about to sneeze. Instead she gave a long pot-stove gurgle and burst out laughing. Still standing on his head, Renard did his best to look dignified. "Off her rocker," he bawled, tapping a digit to his forehead. But madame Renard just pointed at her husband and hooted even louder. I reflected that, if revenge really was a dish that was best consumed cold, the woman who 'no longer provided' would have enough to dine on for quite some time to come.

That evening Renard got busy in the ditch, scraping ice and snow off his beloved motor and bedding her down for the night under one of his wife's best goose-down quilts. With more snow on the way and no sign of tractors – let alone snow ploughs - getting through, it looked set to stay where it was for some time to come.

And now our old, much despised Citroen 2CV came into her own. Built to carry 50 kilos of potatoes, several bulky farmers and the odd, black-arsed pig to market, for the upwardly mobile rural community our 2CV was redolent of mended britches and wooden clogs and all the other humiliations of all too recent rural poverty. Not so long ago everyone in Charente had one. Nowadays, however, it was the far less practical Astras and Vectras bought 'on tick' which squatted sleekly outside every home and Sundays which had once been spent content indoors with the family, were now lavished, disgruntled, on washing the car. And in the freshly fallen snow these sleek machines floundered like dancing buffalos, whereas our 2CV in snow chains sailed over the highest drifts like a feather.

It started with Renard asking if we 'didn't mind' just picking up a few bits and pieces from the village shop. Then Steamy Specs popped by, ogled Fabrice's manly shadow in the shower and asked if we wouldn't mind fetching her heart pills from the chemist's. She was closely followed by *pére* Buissard who needed pellets for his hunting rifle, followed by Granny who couldn't live without her favourite chocolate caramels. By mid-afternoon when we set out to drive the five kilometres to Montemboeuf, we had something to buy for just about everyone in the village.

When we got clear of Mouzon we had difficulty recognising our route. It was the oddest sensation: this road we'd travelled just about every day had become totally unfamiliar. Great drifts of snow bellied out from the fields, effacing the boundary between road and ditch like nature's Tippex. No tyre marks to be seen either. Only the almond-shaped tracks of young roebucks had stirred the snow - and the stubbier pads of ambling badgers. A hawk sat on a fencepost motionless. With his greased back wings and claws as ostentatious as builders muscles the bird was far more suited to this environment than we were - and knew it - and he watched us past with a haughty sneer. Further down the road a gaggle of Partridges sat waiting to be fed. Bred in captivity and released just in time for the hunting season, these birds were so ridiculously tame it would have been easier to strangle them with bare hands. But this would have looked silly in huntsmen's photos, of course, and made for sorry boasting over drinks in the local bars.

Like stiff, white toilet brushes the laden pine branches lined our route. From time, to time the soughing wind grazed through and made them drop their snowy charge with the satisfying sound of strawberries falling into a pot of creamy paint. Everything looked so different. We could have been swanning round Sweden in sub-zero temperatures, or mooching round Moscow in -12 celcius. It was like meeting an old friend who'd had plastic surgery - there was something terribly familiar about the face of this countryside, but nothing we could quite place.

It took us nearly an hour to do a journey which usually took us ten minutes and when we finally arrived in Montemboeuf the main street looked like the aftermath of a wild bumper-car party. Pavements were cluttered with cars which had crashed into each other and expired and the verges were strewn with vehicles which had slewed off the road and been abandoned. In the centre of this mechanical mayhem the tiny Co-op was doing brisk business. Coming in from the Wild North we half expected to see trappers dragging bearskins through the doorway, or Eskimos tripping through the aisles followed by packs of docile seals. Instead the shop was full of harassed housewives who bulldozed up and down the aisles with trolleys full of shopping, trailing snotty-nosed, whimpering kids whose frozen mitts were full of boxes of

107

washing powder and bottles of bleach and anything else that mamma's trolley couldn't handle. Even the - usually glib - grocer was a shadow of his former self. He was used to having one customer per-hour and plenty of time for tittle-tattle, so how could he cope with these 'strangers' who steamed through his shop, intent on getting the last of whatever was left, before a neighbour-become-deadly-foe got in there and got it first?

Luckily, by the time we got to the checkout things had slackened off a little and the grocer had recovered sufficiently to regale us with his latest tale about what he called, 'those crazy English'. A British couple had bought a holiday house in the area recently and their previous night's antics were all the talk of Montemboeuf. "They were sitting watching a film - something about an explorer suffering with depression the English's wife told the gendarmes - when the English stood up and said he was 'just popping out'," the grocer explained. "A few hours later the English's wife calls up the gendarmerie in a terrible state. Her husband had disappeared and she was sure it had something to do with this film, she said. So the coppers scoured the countryside looking for the English and after several hours hunting they found his car abandoned by the roadside. Fearing the worst they followed his tracks. They led across a snowy field and into a sheep pen. And inside the sheep pen, what do you think they saw?"

Dutifully we shook our heads.

"They saw the English snuggled up between two fat sheep, snoring alike one of your snobby British Lords. The cops said it had almost seemed a shame to wake him." The grocer winked at me. "Ah, you English! Completely crazy you are - every single one of you," he said.

Our triumphant return to Mouzon laden with provisions for the entire village assured our keep for the duration of the freezing weather. To thank us, Granny gave us a sack of mud-jacketed potatoes, Steamy Specs doled out liberal helpings of her bottled *Mojhettes*, Buissard chipped in with half a haunch of sheep from his freezer and even Dédé gave us a dozen bottles of his homemade, gut-rot wine. As for *père* Renard he gave us the best gift of all: he allowed us to filch as much wood as we needed from the huge pile of logs in his barn, for as long as the cold snap lasted - and it probably saved our lives..

Released from immediate petty worries such as starvation and hypothermia, without electricity, or water and cut off from the rest of the world by snow, we spent the next two weeks living at a completely different rhythm. Strapping on cross-country skis each day we spent hours gliding over the fields, exploring this new, white world. Exhausted we returned and fetched water from Renard's well and washed and then baked potatoes over the roaring log fire and ate them, piping hot, by the romantic – and inexpensive - glimmer of candlelight.

And when the snow finally thawed we got a phonecall from some distant relatives of Fabrice's father. They'd heard of our incredibly foolish move and curiosity prompted them to invite us for a meal in their house on the outskirts of Angoulême. The chance of free food was too good to miss, so on the appointed day we managed to squeeze some petrol out of a supply left over for the chainsaw and set out to meet Fabrice's distant relatives, with stomachs rumbling like distant thunder.

Their characterless beige bungalow looked as out of place, in the centre of a hamlet of stone cottages, as a poisonous *Ammanite phalloide* would if you found it in a plate of *Cep* mushrooms. It was the sort of house which resembled a hundred others and since you could easily mistake any of the hundred others for your own, you could just as easily imagine entering another door one night and waking up the following day to find yourself leading someone else's life.

Struck with vague misforgivings, we crossed an impeccably trimmed lawn decorated with plough shares painted shiny black and iron cauldrons planted with purple pansies and entered a lime Formica kitchen lit with neon.

It was de rigueur in Charente to kiss relatives twice on each cheek, but when Fabrice's distant aunt moved in for the greeting clinch her face turned sour. After a brief peck in the air above our - grubby - ears she pulled away and showed us stiffly to the table. The fact was that we stunk. After two months of heating ourselves night and day over an open log fire, our hair - our very skin - was impregnated with the nauseous stench of smoke and Fabrice's distant relatives – who, I noticed, were growing ever more distant by the minute - had the delightful impression that they were dining out with the garden bonfire. We sat gingerly as chairs were shifted abruptly away from us and there were loud sniffing sounds, but with food in the offing pride took a backseat, so we ignored the cool welcome and tucked into our stuffed, braised cabbage like famished vultures. Since talk turned short shortly after the entrée, however, not even we were brazen enough to stick it out beyond dessert. When comments on the utility of soap and the wonders worked by tap water got a bit too pointed to bear, we stuffed a last spoonful of pear flan and with eyes still riveted regretfully on the cheese plate, took our leave. Needless to say we were never invited again.

CHAPTER NINE

After the festive hiatus, the new year 1989 brought us back to earth with a bump. Despite daily phonecalls and regular trips to Angoulême, neither of us could find work. Frustrating interviews terminated in open-ended promises - which just seemed to stay open – as we discovered that we were under-qualified for this job, over-qualified for that one, when (as it was slowly dawning on us) the qualifications we really lacked, were social ones. Jobs out here in the countryside were few and far between and what work there was around, was strictly reserved 'for the boys'. We didn't know the mayor, didn't lunch with the bank director, or have a cousin, who had a cousin on the board of directors. In fact, apart from a very tenuous relationship with a farmer who'd played with Fabrice when he was in nappies, we didn't know anyone at all. We'd got used to being considered as valuable employment assets, neither of us had ever had difficulty finding work. For the first time in our lives we were finding out what it was like to be out of work - of not being able to find work – and it came as a huge shock.

Slowly, sometimes very painfully, we were adapting to this whole new ball game which had become our life – and 'slow', we were discovering to our dismay, was all too often the operative word. Not for nothing were the *Charentais* nicknamed 'snails': everything was complicated and everything took time. 'Act at leisure and then repent at even more leisure' seemed to be the local motto and even a simple act, like changing the address on my *carte de séjour* (a chore which has to be carried out at every single change of address), turned into an unbelievably long-winded nightmare.

At the local town hall, where I presented myself with the previous *carte de séjour*, along with multiple proofs of my identity and a birth certificate mentioning the full names and occupations of members of my family stretching back three generations, large books with iron hasps were consulted, buttons were pressed, mountains of photocopies were made, forms were signed, stamped, and double-stamped – and then I produced my passport photos.

"You have changed your hairstyle!" said the secretary accusingly. She pored over them suspiciously, then phoned up *monsieur le maire*.

There was a heated debate as to whether, in the light of my perfidious locks, I should provide a new set of photos., but I settled the question by pointing out that I could hardly be expected to change my *carte de séjour* every time I went to the hairdressers and faced with such implacable logic the mayor's secretary was obliged - albeit begrudgingly – to concede.

We were here and we intended to stay so we did our best to grit our teeth and get on with it. Even so, there were times when it was hard to remain patient faced with bureaucracy gone berserk. Time, after time we'd drive 35 kilometres to Angoulême clutching vital documents and with a rendezvous to sort out this, or that minor formality, only to be told that the disembodied voice who'd given us an appointment over the phone had got it wrong and the boss, was on holiday, and wouldn't be back until next week. "So couldn't we just see someone else?" we'd plead and be greeted with icy scorn. When the Kingpin was away, whole departments fell into decay. Only the Big White Chief had access to vital dossiers. Only He could tell us how many documents we should produce in order to convince French bureaucracy that we really existed. 'Only He' - would breathe some sycophantic secretary who generally barred access to her Lords domain as if her life depended on it - could give us such sensitive information as: how many photos we should include with our application to change the address on our driver's licenses, or whether it was better to photocopy a *carte de séjour* recto-verso, or on a single-sided sheet, when sending it with the previously cited form.

Caught up in this myriad of petty formalities which made moving, or doing anything, in France a minor nightmare, the temptation was to slam our fists down on the table and create what the French themselves call a *'scandale'*.

One day, hot and frustrated after hours of queuing at the social security office, that's exactly what we did and we were instantly whisked into a plush office, where - although it was not strictly his job, you understand? - an affable under-manager fixed our problem right away.

As we left Fabrice pointed to a line of weary suppliants still waiting to be seen. "Unfortunately here in France bawling your head off is often the only way to get things done," he said wearily and it struck me as highly ironic - to think that this was a country which had had a Revolution and yet the people's representatives were as inaccessible as any of the big-nosed Counts of yesteryear. I remembered France's most famous philosopher, Jean-Paul Sartre, defining the individual as: 'a free agent in a deterministic and seemingly meaningless environment". Anyone who has dealt with French bureaucracy will know exactly what he meant.

We had to face it – we couldn't find work. We talked it over for hours on end. What were we to do? We'd grown used to life in the countryside and didn't want to move back to the town, but how could we survive without work?

Gradually the answer became clear. The only thing we could do was start out own business.

The second question was: what with?

This answer was a little more nebulous. I'd come into a small inheritance which could probably assure us a loan and then maybe there were grants?

Grandly we swept onto the third question: what kind of business?.

The answer quickly materialised. Since I'd been a tour guide in a previous existence and Fabrice had worked as a guide in the Palace of Versailles, tourism was the obvious angle. After all, as tourists ourselves we'd noticed the lack of hotels and leisure facilities in the area and yet it seemed to us that this unspoilt countryside would be a paradise for jaded townies – like us!

A visit to the local tourist office confirmed our budding notion. Scouring the shelves we discovered plenty of glossy documents boasting the charms of the Côte d'Azur, but hardly anything about the Charente area which this office was supposed to promote. It seemed to us that the field was wide open. Everything was just waiting to be done and here *we* were, just waiting to do it, so without more ado we made an appointment to see the Director of Tourism for Charente and one apple-blossom scented afternoon in early Spring,, we set off to meet him in Angoulême.

The first shock upon entering his office was a giant size poster of the Lascoux caves, in Dordogne, pinned above his desk. "We must have come to the wrong office," I panicked.

In guise of reply, Fabrice pointed to an elaborate brass plaque on the leather-top desk in front of us. It read: 'Director of Tourism, Charente'. I stared around the plush bureau seeking clues. There were plenty of posters of pretty ports along the Atlantic coast, there was a beauty bathing on a beach near Cannes and there was even a blow up dummy of the Eiffel Tower, but of *'La Charente'* we'd come to see him about there wasn't the slightest sign. I remembered Samuel Johnson, who'd said that best road in England was the one leading out of it and I mused that everything in the Charente tourist Director's office seemed to be telling us that the best place in Charente, was anywhere but.

His first words confirmed our growing fears. Having listened with a heard-it-all-before expression to our plans to open a Guest house and offer guided tours of the surrounding area, he just yawned. "I'm afraid there is no tourism in Charente," he said.

I stared at him. "I'm sorry?"

"Je vous en prie," he said, as if I'd apologised for burping.

"No, I mean 'm sorry I must have misheard you - you are telling us that there are no large structures for tourists in Charente at the present time, perhaps?"

He shook his head. "I mean there is no tourism," he said flatly and then he rubbed his fingernails on the back of his sleeve, then he sighed as if he was sick to the back teeth of spending his days rendezvousing with ignorant imbeciles and added, "No wun wanna spend 'olidays 'ere. *Comprendo?*" in his best pidgin-Esperanto.

In a state of vague shock, I studied his face. He had thick jowls, dissipated skin and those tired-lidded, see-through-you sort-of eyes that belong to people who spend their lives rustling bits of paper and dispensing favours which – according to the current democratic ethos - are not even theirs to dispense. I looked at his costly brass plaque again just to make sure, then fixed his pinched face and stifled an urge to bellow: "Well if there's no bloody tourism in Charente, what the hell do *you* do all day?" Then a faint hope occurred to me - perhaps this wasn't really the Director of tourism in Charente, at all? Perhaps the real Director had been taken ill and this was just his stand-in? I summoned up the courage to ask his name.

He looked instant death at me down a nose that genetics, or a skilful plastic surgeon, had copied from similar nose-jobs found on old paintings hung in desecrated halls and representing mostly degenerate - mainly decapitated – aristocrats and pointing to his costly name plaque, he said scornfully, "My dear madam, isn't it obvious that I, am He?"

So I gave up and left Fabrice to pick up the gauntlet. His mission was to convince Charente's august tourist director that there might indeed be tourism here in Charente. "Here in Charente," Fabrice began auspiciously – and the mere mention of that 'C' word set the director bridling like a nun at a skunk - "we have some of the best preserved roman baths in Europe," he finished.

"Pshahh!" gasped *Monsieur le Directeur*

"And there's the Touvre, which is second largest resurgence in France," said Fabrice.

"Poowuh!" sneered our interlocutor.

"And there are caves here, just like in the Perigord," Fabrice added, pointing to the glossy Dordogne poster above his head.

For all reply the Director of Charente tourism muttered a vulgar French equivalent of teaching Grannies to suck eggs – only where things other than eggs were being aspirated - and said: "If you wish to discuss caves you must make a rendezvous with *Monsieur la Grotte* at the Department of Archaeology," and then he stood up, signalling that the interview was at an end.

He'd reckoned without Fabrice, however. Apart from being about as easy to fob off as Smollet's famed 'French friend' who: "..pushes your patience to the limit with his prolonged visits and - far from seizing the most precise allusions to his leave-taking - comments that you seem down-hearted and he will keep you company," Fabrice had a rhino-hide when it came to taking hints, plus a multitude of ploys designed to confound the most erudite conversational adversary, one of which consisted in hopping from topic, to topic without providing any apparent form of link. He employed this devastating tactic on Charente's Director now. "And what about lakes?" he said, remaining firmly seated.

Bewilderment flitted like mist across the Director's pallid face.

"To swim in!" bellowed Fabrice.

Charente's representative found his feet once more. "People who want to swim go to the seaside," he said haughtily and in a single phrase he laid bare to us the depressing vista of what 'tourism' was to him.

Like a series of amateur snapshots (the stills of his limited imagination) I saw queues for horns of shellfish and sand grinding teeth to a fine edge in the picnic baguette. There were sardines turning lobster on overcrowded beaches, whining kids knocking over sandcastles and torturing jellyfish and old men taking their pot-bellies on a post-prandial stroll to digest skimpy bikinis by the sea For him this was what tourism was all about. For him this was what the masses wanted - and since we were talking masses, it went without saying that his idea of what constituted 'successful tourism' was measured out in kilos of vacationing meat.

So he imagined these gaudy postcard scenes and represented them as the pinnacle of any Tourist Director's career. In his wildest dreams as head of tourism for all of France, he saw himself sat in a luxurious office cut off from the real world, being nurtured by a big-breasted women – the sort you saw on St Tropez postcards - who soothed his brow as it burnt with savant holiday-industry calculations, such as the amount of punters you could cram on the Mont-St-Michel in a single day whilst maintaining unprofitable, but, alas, essential breathing space, or the number of days that punters could be expected to queue for the Louvre, without being offered bed and board.

Not that he'd ever be caught doing any of these hideous things himself, of course. But that was quite besides the point. He was merely an instrument appointed by God - and his associates on the *Conseil Général* - to give the punters what they really wanted and since what they wanted was this thing called 'tourism' and since tourism was this, the rest was just matter of simple mathematics - and never mind what you said about tourists who'd already visited the Charente area. Why, anyone could see they weren't the real thing at all. They had walking shoes, when everyone knows tourists hobble about in crippling sandals. They wore sensible pullovers, when everyone knows tourists wear skimpy skirts and 'kiss-me-quick' hats. They didn't have dollars oozing from their wallets, or cameras strung round their necks and they'd never been heard to say stupid things like: "take a picture and I'll look at it when I get back home." In short they did not correspond to his preconceived image of the average tourist and therefore they simply did not exist. "Here we only have trees and cows and they're of no interest to anyone," he concluded, dismissing the subject of tourism in Charente, like a parent tells a child: "I said 'no', and that's the end of it." Then he showed us to the door.

Outside his office I shook my head in despair. "You'd think he hated us for even mentioning there could be tourism here," I said wonderingly.

"I wouldn't take it personally. He'll have forgotten all about us in five minutes," came Fabrice's soothing reply.

"He might forget all about us, but I don't think I'll forget him in a hurry," came my rattled response.

CHAPTER TEN

Spring came early that year and it was a blessed relief for us. Like seriously overweight squirrels we slowly emerged from hibernation. By the end of March we were out from under rolls of woolly jumpers and itchy scarves. By mid-April we'd even ditched the bulging long-johns and vests like the ones our mother's used to make us wear, and started to remember the simple things in life, like skin. As the days grew longer, the light grew stronger and leaves sprouted everywhere - even out of the logs we threw on the fire - gradually the stale, accumulated odours of winter started to fade and the green-grass smells of spring came filtering in, via the wide-open front door.

On balmy evenings, as ghostly owls chased mice in the fields and warmth rising from the tarmac brought Pipistrels to swoop and seek insects along the corridor of road, high up at his window in the house overlooking the church square the *'petit fou's'* elder brother, Lulu, serenaded the village with tunes extracted, note by note, from his battered red squeezebox. 'The Chicken Dance' had just hit Charente and several times each evening we were treated to his wheezy version of the catchy little ditty. *"C'est la danse des oiseaux. C'est la danse des oiseaux. La, la, la, la. Qua, qua, qua, qua,"* we'd hear his accordion whine and sneeze and if we poked noses out of doors it was to see Dédé, or *père* Buissard - who 'just happened to be passing' - suddenly double up and splay their feet and bob and weave, wheeze and gasp, as they did the 'Chicken Dance', just like they'd seen it done on Saturday evening TV. High above them Lulu pumped on oblivious, as if this nightly hob-nail footed homage was nothing more than his rightly due.

Evenings grew warmer still. The last daffodil vanished from newly ploughed gardens and cowslips started to spring up on sun-dappled forest paths and in bright emerald fields. With the warmer weather Lulu's thoughts turned to love and soon the amorous strains of Edith Piaf's, *'La Vie en Rose'*, rent the air or, on evenings when he was all alone - when the orange street lamps had been snuffed out like candles and night fell as soft as suede on skin - it was the haunting tune of Jacques Brel's, *'Ne me quitte pas'* which insinuated it's way past closed shutters and lace curtains, like a mournful reproach to anyone who'd ever contemplated leaving anyone, at anytime, anywhere.

Most nights, however, Lulu's brother, the *'fou'*, returned from guarding cows, or cutting grass, around 8pm and the squeezebox was abandoned whilst the Maestro got busy with pots and pans. After a suitable pause for ingurgitation and the briefest segue for digestion, however, the concert generally resumed. Unfortunately 'the food of love' was often forced to declare forfeit to wine out of five-litre plastic bottles and the *soirée* generally staggered to a cacophonic climax which had the entire village screaming for ear plugs, before ending in a more harmonious concert of snores.

Lulu and the *'fou'* were one of Mouzon's major landmarks. The odd couple had lived together in the big old house by the church ever since anyone could remember - and they'd lived alone together since way back in 1953, when their mother died of consumption. They were a part of Mouzon's history and yet the wildest rumours still circulated about the pair. Employed by the mayor to do all the village odd-jobs, everyone knew it was the *'fou'* who bought money into the house, whilst Lulu stayed at home, prepared the meals and did all the other household chores - even, it was said in prurient whispers, cobbling his brother's socks! The word 'exploitation' was often muttered in connection with the two brothers: there were some who said - although never to his face - that Lulu was like a pimp who sent his simpleton brother out, like a prostitute, to earn money, whilst he stayed at home and lived a life of wanton ease on these ill-gotten gains. Another titillating piece of gossip made much of the brother's sleeping arrangements: the words 'one double bed', figured largely in these whispered conversations. Luckily the rumours hardly bothered the pair - hadn't they been hearing the same old tittle-tattle, over and over, for the past 40 years? Recently, however, something had happened which bothered them very much. After a lifetime in the big old house by the church, the mayor had announced that he intended to re-house them.

Ostensibly the mayor had said it was for the brother's good and he'd cited the lack of facilities, such as running water, or plumbing, as proof of his good faith. Unfortunately for the mayor, however, old friend rumour had been hard at work and the bother's suspected that the real reason behind the projected move, was plain, faithless greed. It seemed that *monsieur le maire* had woken up to the potential of the big old house by the church one sunny morning and now he wanted to turn the brother's home into Gîtes for wealthy Parisians, in order to generate loads of money to subsidise new toilets for the village bar, as well as plenty of long, liquid, lunches. For 40 years the brothers had paid a ridiculously low rent to live in the big old house and now it was time, the mayor said, for them to live somewhere a bit more modest. He'd suggested a two-roomed bungalow on the edge of the village, overlooking the cemetery. Lulu and the 'fou' refused to budge, however, so the exasperated village authority sent a host of minor officials to pester them into submission. These suited, booted bureaucrats came rapping at the door at siesta time, when Lulu was still groggy from sleep and tried to bully him into signing forms studded with long words he didn't understand, like 'dispossession' and 'expropriation'. After a few months of this, Lulu just stopped answering the door. Then he tried enlisting support from other villagers, but no-one wanted to go against the mayor. *"On n'y peut rien,"* they said, when he tried to rally them to his cause and then they sighed heavily, as if to say that, although their hands were tied, their hearts were firmly with Lulu and the *'fou'*. Hoping to enlist our support for his lonely cause, one morning in early may Lulu invited us round to visit his abode.

Six, or seven, hundred years ago the ancient presbytery must have been a magnificent dwelling - as we followed Lulu up endless flights of stairs and along never-ending corridors, we caught glimpses of vast, echoing rooms, with vaulted ceilings as distant as the sky, whose walls were studded with lighter patches which spoke of an - erstwhile extensive - portrait gallery. There were intricately carved pillars and elaborately painted frescoes. There was a whole room panelled from floor-to-ceiling in sumptuous mahogany and another one covered in mirrors. But most of the windows were broken now, there were zinc buckets full of rain water on every landing, the sumptuous oak floorboards were shot to bits by woodworm and the distant ceilings were festooned with dry rot fungi.

We followed Lulu through to the single room he and his brother shared, right at the heart of this baroque hovel. Their bedroom/kitchen/living space, alone, was the size of an average factory floor. Far away at the other end of the long room we caught a glimpse of the infamous double bed. Above it hung a fly-stained photo of a much younger Lulu playing the trumpet, next to it was a picture of the *'fou'* in blue, work overalls and next to that was a faded photo of a woman in her late forties. She was as plump as a Botero painting and sported a black hat squashed down at a jaunty angle, over a round head encased in ringlets. This, I guessed, must be the pair's long-dead mother.

Opposite the infamous bed, at the other end of the long room, there was a spotted gas ring. Next to it, on a small dresser, were a few, charred pots and pans. There were two, large windows in the room, but neither of them gave any light. Most of the panes were broken and patched up with dark brown cardboard. There was a fire burning in a vast grate, some of the *'fou's'* blue work overalls hanging from a rusted nail by the door and a table made of planks in the centre of the room. A tumbler containing a few sprigs of sweet-smelling honeysuckle stood on this table, beside a crusty loaf of bread and a bottle of the local homemade gut-rot, known as *'Gnole'*. Under the table there was a bucket full of dirty plates and soiled forks waiting to be taken down to the well and washed.

We stared around us in utter amazement. It was like being in some grand mansion that had been commandeered for stationing troops, then abandoned. The air of neglect, the lack of comfort, was almost inconceivable and yet Lulu showed us around the grimy hovel with the grandest airs. And when I ventured to ask him if he didn't think they'd be better off in the modern bungalow, with all 'mod-cons' by the cemetery, he was quite offended. What did it matter if there was no running water or plumbing? Who cared if he had to wash his clothes on a stone by the stream in the garden, or use a toilet which was outside in the garden, near the veg patch? He'd lived in this big old house, by the church and overlooking the village square, all his life. For him this derelict old manor was 'home'.

When we left him he was ranting that if the mayor wanted to get him and his brother to leave, he'd have to take them out in a wooden box. The Gods must have been listening because a week later the *'petit fou'* was killed.

All that fateful morning a wind of folly had been blowing over the village. It was the day of the annual hunters dinner and a special battue had been organised in honour of this grand event. Since 7am we'd heard horns blasting and shots fired on the village square and by 8am, when the *'fou'* had struggled sleepily out of bed to ring the church bells, his snores had been drowned out by all the noise and Dédé was half an hour late in climbing the tower to pull him down.

By 9am the bar was chock-a-block with hunters and sleepy Mouzon had become as murderous as war-torn Vietnam. Men clad in green camouflage trousers and caps with rabbity ear flaps and war reporter's multi-pocket jackets - and some even streaked with green camouflage paint – clomped in and out in steel-capped boots, looking purposeful, toting mean looking weapons and discussing strategy as they consumed inordinate amounts of homemade *'Gnole'*. Lulu didn't hunt - and the *'fou'* wasn't considered capable - but at 10am the two of them crept into the bar, anyway, and just before the hunters set out to wage war on the local wildlife, they stood in one corner an basked in a few, sweet instants of reflected glory. Ten minutes later 40 inebriated huntsmen - and four-score dogs who were just as tipsy with unaccustomed freedom - set out to affront the redoubtable enemy, whilst Lulu returned to his oven to sweat over Sunday lunch - and the *'fou'* just disappeared.

Later, they said it wasn't possible that the *'fou'* had had the idea all on his own. Later, they said it was Dédé who must have whispered that it would be a fine joke to sneak on ahead of the rowdy group and hide in a bush, then leap out on them roaring like a wild boar.

Hearing the first shots Granny and *père* Renard rubbed their hands, anticipating the magnificent boar stew they would eat in the village hall that night. But the bedraggled huntsmen returned, an hour later, not victorious with a boar on a spit, but ridiculous, with the lifeless *'fou'* on a stretcher.

CHAPTER ELEVEN

I have heard it said that the most successful Estate agents have '666' tattooed at the base of their neck and may possess a sixth finger. Other warning signs are said to be large moles in strange places and the unnerving habit of murmuring odd invocations – words like: 'Trust me! Trust me!' - as they reach out to shake hands on the clincher. Burning the devil's accomplices – and some would say, unfortunately - went out of fashion a while ago, however and these days Estate agents and their fiendish ilk, are free to roam the French countryside preying on their favourite victims, who are generally foreigners out to buy their dream homes in a single weekend.

According to the best-loved apocryphal tales – all of which you're sure to hear if you ever decide to buy a house in France - the ideal victim won't speak French, but has read all the books about what to do when buying. Having studied chapter three about 'not purchasing the first house you see,' he will insist on seeing ten properties a day - even though he has backache and blisters by the third visit – and despite his aching limbs, he will poke about in the loft for hours on end, looking for suspicious piles of sawdust (see chapter six about 'termites') and asking about dry rot with the 'dry-rot' expression of one who's seen it all before, because he's read chapter nine about 'trying to look knowledgeable'.

Unfortunately for the victim, Roger has read all the books as well - plus a few more about elemental human psychology. Roger is that irrational 'human element' which books about 'the right way to do things' just never seem to take into account. Roger is the victim's Estate agent.

Bland, not to say oleaginous, Roger will give the victim exactly what he wants. He will answer all his questions – almost before they are formulated – and will even have a slick response for that complicated question about 'rights of way'. He will let slip bits of knowledge which demonstrate his fabulous command of DIY *parleyvoo*, will casually let slip that he 'knows a good builder' and will almost *always* compliment the victim on his command of the French lingo, when the victim's so-called 'command' is almost *always* non-existent. Once the victim is eating out of Roger's

135

sweaty palm as blithely as a pigeon in St Mark's square, bland, unassuming, friendly, nice-guy Roger will smile obsequiously and invite his prey to join him and partake of 'some grub and a bit of plonk', in the local café.

If this was a horror movie there would be a red triangle flashing on and off the screen at this point, and a student on BBC work-experience would be running his fingernails up and down a school blackboard. Unfortunately this isn't a horror movie, this is the horror of real life and instead of getting the hell out of there while the going's good, after weakly protesting: "back home I usually grab a sandwich", the victim will meekly follow the Roger into the crowded, local bar.

And so it is that, all because he skipped that vital chapter 25, about the dangers of long, liquid lunches, having dodged all the pitfalls mentioned in all the manuals, the victim falls foul to the biggest booby trap of all. And so it is that, bathed in a roseate haze of cheap alcohol, cradled by talk of vast swimming pools and cocooned by exciting possibilities of buying-up-extra-acres-and-thus-assuring-total-privacy, he will find himself signing contracts, that should have been studied under crude lighting, by lawyers 'back home', with inebriated brio on the corner of a wine-stained table, somewhere in the heart of France.

The next sequence takes place a few months later, when the victim and his – apocryphal - family have taken up residence. The house will seem a lot smaller than Roger's prey remembered it and he will discover he has neighbours who have half-a-dozen hunting dogs, which are kept in a stinking two-by-four pen just beneath his kitchen window. But never mind. He has decided to make the best of it. He is in another country now and must learn to *'vivre'* and *'laissez vivre'*, he will lecture his apocryphal wife.

Gradually the victim will settle into his new dwelling - although the words 'back home' will insinuate themselves with increasing frequency into the most anodyne of conversations, about the most anodyne matters, i.e., food: "France might be the home of the Galloping Gourmet, but they make bloody lousy baked beans", or building materials: "I don't know what it is about their paint, but it just isn't as white as ours."

If the victim is called 'Carpenter' he will proudly baptise his new home, *'Chez le Menuisier'* and be bugged for weeks with phonecalls about spiral staircases. 'The Blacks' will inevitably call their place *'Chez Les Noirs'* and be subject to racist attacks and as for 'The Whites', they will be clever and call their house *'Mont Blanc,'* and have to explain the pun forever after..

And just when the garden is looking exactly the way the victim wanted it and he's got the sort-of all-over tan which will be the envy of friends back home, Roger's unsuspecting prey will discover that his new home is in the centre of the proposed route for a four-lane motorway and his ever-so-helpful Estate agent has lit out for Paraguay.

Seeing us browsing in her shop window in Montbron, the Estate agent leapt out and dragged us inside and when we told her we were looking for a house with lots of large rooms, loads of character, a good roof and not much work to be done, she rubbed her hands. "Are you planning to open a guesthouse?" she asked.

We nodded.

She purred with satisfaction and pulled out a leather bound dossier. Prices started at 750,000 francs and spiralled rapidly upwards.

Taking his cue from my gasp of horror, Fabrice shook his head. "Cheaper," he said.

Slightly disgruntled she pulled out a sheaf of cardboard and showed us several, elegant clichés of houses starting at 500,000 francs.

I hiccupped loudly. "Cheaper," said Fabrice.

She coughed and muttered something about getting blood from stones, but after fiddling in her drawer she produced

a swathe of dingier photos. 350,000 francs was the average price ticket.

This time when I giggled nervously and Fabrice said 'cheaper', she repeated the word, snapping it in two like a brittle twig. Totally impervious, Fabrice maintained eye contact. The estate agent grunted. Like many before her, she was unnerved by his bald cheek. She rummaged about in a filing cabinet and held up a faded, black-and-white photo of a gigantic ruin which had survived the Hundred Years War, but only just. 250,000 francs, was the asking price here.

Fabrice opened his mouth. "Chhhh," he began.

The agent put her finger to her lips. "Shhh!" she said, and showed us firmly to the door.

Together we'd calculated we could afford 150,000 francs to buy a house, 230,000 francs for conversion work and 50,000francs for furniture and other fittings.

"You'll never do it," said Fabrice's family, my friends, our new neighbours - and even the dustbin man. It was as if they all had a vested interest in seeing us fail.

Unperturbed we calculated we needed a total of 430,000 francs. Two-thirds of this we knew we could borrow from the bank, but only if we provided the remaining third up-front. A rapid subdivision said we had to find 150,000 francs. My small inheritance added up to 75,000 francs, which left another 75,000 francs to find. We decided to look into the possibility of getting a grant - first of all, did one exist?

"Yes," said the Chamber of Commerce. "No", opined the Prefecture. "Definitely not!" said an outraged female from the Chamber of Industry and then a friend of hers, a representative from the Chamber of Agriculture told us there might be if we became farmers. It was like some game of administrative Badminton and we were the human shuttlecocks. Everybody had different opinions, all of which were given at great length, but nobody seemed to know anything for sure. It was our first encounter with what the French themselves called *'m'enfoutisme'*, which roughly translates as a gallic version of the old British catchphrase: "It's more than my job's worth", topped up with the very French refrain of: "and I wouldn't care even if it wasn't!"

"Why on earth should the State pour money into your pockets?" demanded a hard-faced representative of the regional tourist board. She made us feel like we were criminals. We were beginning to understand that 'entrepreneur' was a dirty word here in France. There were thousands of non-profit making 'associations' here - and millions of francs were doled out to them in grants every year. If we'd have belonged to one of them we would have been treated with great solicitude and been offered an office and a telephone in the local town hall. Unfortunately we were 'private enterprise' and – as we were discovering to our cost - private enterprise was viewed with - almost pathological - suspicion. We were *privées*, we didn't want to do it as a group, we wanted to 'go it alone' and that made us direct descendants of all those calculating Kings and crooked Counts the revolution got rid of. As entrepreneurs we were of the race of the exploiters - and no doubt we preferred using the snobby *'vous'*, rather than the good old, back-slapping, *'tu'*, in our conversations. In short, we were everything that France had ever revolted against and this woman, at least, really seemed to hate our guts.

Once again we were firmly shown to the door. I was getting good at walking backwards without falling over. "Thank you very much Madame Baubon," I said as we left. Her eyes narrowed and she slammed the door shut in my face.

You did that on purpose!" Fabrice guffawed.

"Did what on purpose?"

"Called her 'Baubon'. You know very well that her name is 'Bourbon'."

I was still hot under the collar from our recent interview. "Bourbon, Baubon, what's the bloody difference?" I said irritably.

Fabrice sniggered. "There's a very big one. You see, in French slang the word *'baubon'* means 'prick'."

I stared at him aghast. "You mean I just called her..?"

He nodded gleefully "You just called her 'Madame Prick'," he said.

Round and round and round we went. Financial imperatives meant we needed to get our guesthouse up and running as soon as possible. A cast-iron rule for receiving a grant, however, said that if we bought a property and started renovation work, we'd no longer be eligible for a grant. What's more we needed a grant agreement to persuade the bank to give us a loan to buy the house and renovate. So we jumped back on the crazy administrative carousel and round and round and round we went.

We soon realised that our appearance was a major stumbling block. In order to be considered as entrepreneurs we had to look the part and ponder on weighty things. Kitted out in gear from the

Red Cross and mainly pondering on how to pay the electricity bill, we couldn't possibly be taken seriously, it seemed.

The President of the Gites association gave a careless shrug. A grant may exist, but we did not have - how should he put it? - quite the right profile. He gave us to understand that youth was a major drawback to having a Chambres d'Hôtes and that only people over 60 years old ever set up guesthouses in Charente. He also hinted that — since I was an *Anglaise*, n'est-ce pas? - that if a grant was forthcoming, I might just take the money and run.

A visit to our *'conseiller'* from the *Conseil Générale*, shed some light on the attitudes of local authorities. "They are suspicious of entrepreneurs, because they've been duped too many times in the past," he told us and he gave us a list of projects, which had been funded with State money and ended in disaster. The most recent to date was a bat-eared scheme called 'Leisure Valley'. It was the dream child of an ex-hippy with leather trousers and a pony tail, who arrived in Charente behind the wheel of a pink Cadillac. He'd purchased a field the size of a pocket-handkerchief, with a pond in the middle and - on paper at least - managed to cram in something for everyone. There were jet skis for the intrepid and fishing for the insipid, an inflatable swimming pool for wailing kids, deck chairs for ailing grannies and buggies available to anyone crazy

143

enough to hire them. Although he hailed from Paris, ex-hippy's father had been a local bigwig, so State money was poured into this ill-advised venture. The harrowing mess on 'Day One' is easy to imagine. Jet skis amputated fishing lines, buggies veered into deckchairs, kids and grannies fell into the pond clutching each other and thugs burnt holes, with fags, in the inflatable pool. After a couple of days the park was closed down by 'Health and Safety', and the State-funded buggies and expensive jet skis were left to rot, along with the deflated pool, in fast-growing undergrowth. We were paying for the mistakes of others, it seemed.

More than once I decided to give up the whole idea and go back to my well-paid job in town. But if I was utterly bewildered by - all too often, hostile - attitudes to our project, Fabrice was undaunted and gave me the courage to pick myself up and plug on. It must be said it was easy enough for me: I was the fool who'd waded in where angels feared to tread. I'd just decided I wanted to set up a business in rural France, but I had no idea what I was letting myself in for. I was still naïve enough to think that France was Europe and therefore, apart from enough difference to spice things up a bit, basic attitudes would be much the same as in Britain. But for Fabrice it was totally different. He was well-versed in dealing with French officialdom and he knew what a hard slog we had ahead of us, but he kept on going just the same. When we reached the point where we'd seen everyone in Charente and still had no idea if it was possible to get a grant, for him the choice was instantly apparent: accept to have all our hopes and plans shot down by the snipers of *'m'enfoutisme'*, or decide to put up a fight. That afternoon he called the *monsieur le Président* of tourism for the entire Poitou-Charentes region, himself and arranged us a rendezvous. The following day we scraped up enough money to put petrol in our old banger and drove the hundred, or so, kilometres to Poitiers.

After months of being chucked out of successive offices with very little ceremony, it was a huge relief, when we entered his bureau, to see we'd finally knocked on the right door. Gone were the posters of Dordogne and Denmark - the President's walls were actually lined with crisp, colour images of the area he'd been instated to represent. He was young and dynamic and he listened to our sorry tale with interest, flicked through our carefully prepared dossier and promised he would help.

By now it was mid-summer and we were suspended from action by *les vacances*, as we waited to hear about the grant. Shops and businesses shut for holidays as the French invested their beaches and secondary homes. So we learnt to take our time as well. On days when the skies were bleached blue-peroxide, when it was hot enough to fry an egg on a stone and even Jiminy and his band of crickets were playing it drowsy, we went to Lavaud's newly built lake and picnicked and bathed, or rolled like wet dogs scratching fleas, in the long, silky grass. Once, or twice a snake zig-zagged past us, on his way to the opposite bank and one lunchtime we spied a stag, who frolicked in the heat-oiled water like a frisky puppy. Apart from that we were alone in the world. There was only the wide, blue sky, the deep green lake, a bottle green fringe of pine trees, a few russet cows and an occasional heron and sometimes we just stripped off all our clothes and plunged, naked, into the blood-warm waters.. We swam and sunbathed, siesta'd and took strolls and we no longer asked ourselves if we'd done the right thing, because we *knew* we'd done the right thing..

And after a long, lazy summer, the exciting news arrived in September. Impressed with our exposé and interested by our scheme, the President of Poitou-Charentes tourism had pulled all the strings within reach. Thanks to him we were to be awarded 65,000 Francs - the maximum grant accorded for this kind of project. Of course we were overjoyed. We didn't realise it then, but by taking the initiative and going directly to the President, we'd gone over the heads of half-a-dozen local bigwigs and - all unwitting - made a heckuva lot of enemies..

CHAPTER TWELVE

The very next day after receiving news about the grant, Fabrice started putting the word out. In shops, in banks, in queues at the bakers - and even whilst waiting at a pedestrian crossing, he entered into long conversations, which ended with him handing out bits of paper with our phone number on it.

Each time, as he described the vast mansion we wanted to buy for hardly any money, I went crimson with embarrassment. "Do you have to tell everyone how little money we've got," I'd snarl, as we walked away.

Each time, he would turn and stare at me in amazement. "Well we want to find a house, don't we?" he'd say.

And of course we did. So I was left speechless. After all, how could I explain? How could a Frenchman possibly understand someone who'd been brought up to think that talking about money was vulgar. How could he comprehend a feeble idiot who came out in a bright red rash every time he mentioned the lack of zeros in our bank account? Out here no-one was in the least surprised at his direct methods - and what's more, everyone said they thought they might just know someone, who knew someone else, who just might.. And so the slips of paper were steadily handed out. But it was only when a slip of paper with a scribbled address on it, slithered under our door one day, that it occurred to me this word-of-mouth system, which I'd dismissed out-of-hand as 'ridiculously antiquated', might actually work.

First we took at a look on my marmalade-stained map. The scribbled address corresponded to a tiny village on the Charente/Dordogne border, near enough to the main road to attract seasonal traffic, but far enough away from the motorway to avoid exhaust fumes. It seemed interesting. We decided to take a look.

Renard shook his head when I mentioned the name of the village. "The mayor has right-wing tendencies and doesn't give a hang for outsiders," he said.

I listened with half an ear. After all, it was a house we wanted to buy, not the mayor, or his right-wing sympathies.

So, with the sun at it's zenith, we arrived above a tiny village tumbling down the side of a sloping valley like a Niagara of red-tiled roofs. At the bottom of this steep-sloping bowl, the valley was cut asunder by a meandering river. Long-haired weeping willows linked above it and bent to see their reflections in the water, like a narcissistic rugby scrum. At first sight the village of Vibrac was decidedly picturesque.

We parked the car on a piece of flat land, by a sweet-smelling pine tree and meandered slowly down a narrow lane, into the village. All the newer bungalows had been kept to the crown of the hill, so the further we descended the older the houses seemed to get. It was a hot day in early June and yet wisps of smoke curled from a dozen chimney stacks, giving us a good idea of the average age of the hamlet's inhabitants.

Nosily we peered though open barn doors. We saw high stacks of oak wood and Asterix-plaited tresses of garlic. There were beans hung to dry, which rustled in the soft breeze like paper chimes and funnels on iron legs, which were beetroot presses, and well-honed scythes, hung next to sweet-smelling hay stacked in tall, bushy tufts.

We stopped to sniff at a clump of old fashioned red roses which smelt like the savour of Parma violet sweets. It was one in the afternoon and everyone was indoors, out of the heat, and eating lunch. The French would have said, "*Il n'y a pas un chat,*" but in reality there were plenty of them. There were brown moggies scratching their ears and inspecting their nails, there were marmalade tabbies spread like carpets to dry in the sun and there were tortoise-shell kittens who chased each other's stripy tails up and down the crumbling walls. Hung in baskets, or planted in earthenware pots, besides them were the sempiternal geraniums. There were also thick-scented petunias, who couldn't stand the heat and panted flat out in their window boxes, like flabby purple tongues. Vines trailed along garden gates and tendrils of purple wisteria and pink clematis gave stone-flagged terraces their shade. We saw wicker baskets full of carrots and netting spread over vivid, scarlet strawberry beds. There were sour odours of fresh-sawn wood and pine needles, and sweeter smells of honeysuckle and new-mown grass and thyme. There were bees buzzing above us in the Virginia creeper, there were crickets in the meadows winding up an entire battery of clockwork toys and there was a thick, oak forest, which coiled around it all like a kangaroo's pouch.

We smiled at each other nervously, bitten by that buzz of excitement which tells you 'you're onto something'. We were standing on a dusty square, now, next to a honey-coloured hunk of church. In front of us was the stream we'd seen from above.

Weeds trailed in the lazy water like mouldered hair. We crossed it on a narrow bridge and arrived outside the house - which was more like two houses that had been stuck together in the middle.

One part had served for the owner's business, spinning and dying wool and the other part was the shop where they'd sold knitted cardigans and woolly socks. Once-upon-a-time sheep must have grazed in the pitiful strip of garden. It was littered with beer cans and fag butts now. Once-upon-a-time wool had been washed in the weed-tangled river, then dyed and hung to dry on long poles. Once-upon-a-time, I thought pitying a couple of emaciated willows weeping their hearts out over the current mess.

We entered the main house, which had been shut up ever since the owner's husband was run over by a lumbering cattle truck and found ourselves in a rabbit warren. Up and downstairs we went, opening one door and then another, until we'd lost all sense of orientation. I counted: there were 13 rooms in all. "Unlucky for some," joked Fabrice.

One room was stacked high with bales of wool, dyed stained-glass hues of blue and cochineal and covered in dust. In another room we found the vegetable dyes that had been used to tint the wool, inadvertently stepped into the brightly coloured piles and trailed blue and mauve powder all around the house. We found a spinning wheel that was like something out of a fairy tale, cute thirties posters advertising Phildar woollies and a room that was panelled from top to bottom with wooden cupboards, which opened to reveal evil-looking butchers hooks and said this must have been the family's cold store. There were more store houses, an attic, a hangar, a workshop, stables, outhouses, more buildings, a cellar - and even an inside well - and everywhere there was the accumulated dust and rubbish of a house that had been shut up for three, long decades. Finally, dazed and vaguely exhausted we wandered outside. After the gloom the light was blinding. We'd lost track of the time - the sun had slid almost to the horizon, which meant we'd been in the house for nearly three hours.

As we climbed slowly back up the winding lane, shadows started to paint the countryside black. By the time we reached the top and paused for breath, night had fallen, as snug as a rubber glove, over the dozing village. We stared down into the darkened bowl like crystal gazers, hoping to get a peek at some blissful future where we did all the things we dreamt of with that amazing house. We stared at each other, hardly seeing each other. In our mind's eye we were already hacking off rendering, planting roses and painting walls.. We drove slowly back to Mouzon, wondering if we'd be able to afford our dream.

"Hello is there anyone there?" I said. There was silence except for heavy breathing. Could this be my first ever obscene Charentais phone call, I wondered?

No, it was Madame Fort. After a long pause she said, "I hear you've been looking at other houses."

As soon as we got back from Vibrac we'd phoned her up, only to learn she wanted 270,000 francs for the wool shop by the stream. Regretfully we'd said 'no'. Regretfully we'd started looking at other houses – but we'd counted without the power of the local grapevine.

"So what's wrong with our place then?" said an irate Madame Fort, now. Her voice echoed as if she was holding the receiver half a mile from her mouth.

"Err, nothing," I stammered.

"It's because they're *Anglais!* The *Anglais* don't know a good thing when they see it!" I heard her paralysed husband bawl.

There was a loud crackling as Madame Fort put a hand over the mouthpiece. "Shut up, Jean - they will hear you!" I heard her hiss.

"Pshah! They're *Anglais* and those *Anglais* don't understand a blind word you say!" shrieked the incorrigible Jean. There was a loud crack, as if she'd brained him with the receiver and then silence.

After a while I heard a dog whimper and then several, loud thuds, as if she was clubbing him to death. I leaned into the receiver, fascinated. Sound had separated like oil and water and in the foreground I could hear heavy breathing, whilst a telly droned away in the background. I snatched the phone away from my ear when a fly came into 'view', buzzing like it wanted to break the sonic barrier, then I put it cautiously to my ear again to hear someone on my aural horizon let out a phlegm-filled, death-rattle. I was drawn into the receiver like a radio story, now, as I tried to imagine what was happening at the other end. That rustling noise - as if someone was trying to stuff a starched crinoline frock into the receiver - could that be Madame Fort, who had killed her husband and was now wrapping the body up in a plastic sheet? And what about that repetitive squidgy thud? Could that mean he wasn't quite dead yet and she was having to finish him off?

Finally she came back on line. "I've talked with my husband.. (You can't fool me. I know you're just trying to establish an alibi, I thought) ..and we've decided to lower the price of the house," she said.

It was good news, but not good enough for our micro-budget, so, once again, I politely said 'no', put the 'phone down and thought that would be the end of the matter. It was only the beginning.

Via her secret channels Madame Fort managed to find out each and every time we visited another property - and each and every time I'd get one of her irate phone calls and the price would come down a little more. Which is why, by the end of a month of our constant house visits and her constant phonecalls, we'd earned the reputation of being real hard bargainers - sharks with hearts of stone - when all we'd really done was pick up the phone.

And after two months, without even really meaning to, we'd got the house price reduced by more than half and that's how we found ourselves one misty morning in late September, without even knowing quite how we were going to pay for it, in the notary's office, with Monsieur and Madame Fort, signing a *'sousseing'* to buy their wool shop by a lazy stream.

CHAPTER THIRTEEN

Lucien shot himself the day we left Mouzon.

After the death of the *'fou'* he' seemed to lose his *'raison d'être'*. There were no more socks to darn, no meals to cook and no-one to listen as he wrung tunes from his drunken squeezebox., so it was a simple affair for the mayor to shoehorn him out of the big old house by the church and into the new bungalow with all 'mod-cons', overlooking the graveyard. Lulu had been used to being the centre of life on Mouzon's village square and he'd always been the first to know everything that was going on. Stuffed away out of sight behind the cemetery, he was out of touch with village life and slowly started to go out of his mind.

"Dead men don't tell lies," say a host of Spaghetti Westerns - for whom life's little grey zones are as much a mystery as the grey cells of most of their spectators - but if one wanted to take the glaringly obvious homily a little further, one could add that they

157

don't run off with the post lady, or get drunk and bury an axe in the mayor's door, or do any of the other scandalous little things which lend the welcome spice of gossip to that dull dish which is most people's lives, either. Perhaps a few burials might have livened things up a bit. Perhaps the whistling gravediggers, the gossiping priest and the scandals over a freshly dug grave would have given Lulu a bit of grist for gossip's mill, but not even death would oblige. The Grim Reaper had sent out plenty of calling cards during the hot, summer months, alright - and few of his invitations had been declined – but the season had petered out, as it did every year, in time for a flurry of autumn weddings. The time for dallying near the Styx was over for the moment. Apart from the occasional visitor who came bearing flowers, Lulu's next-door-neighbours were as boringly quiet as – well, as the grave!

Since Granny's was the next house down from the square, she naturally assumed Lulu's role as village chronicler. It was Granny who broke the news that the wife of local builder, Lourdaud, had left him for a man in a tatty, yellow post van. It was Granny - with the aid of Buissard's binoculars - who spotted Renard in a field with Steamy Specs and it was Granny who revealed that Dédé had taken to herding his cows clad in a short skirt and a pair of women's silk stockings. Once upon a time all these juicy scoops of tattle, would have been Lulu's rightful due. These days, however, he just didn't seem interested.

One morning he forgot to ring the church bell - although he'd done it every day since the *'fou'* died. Then he forgot two days running and Dédé, who still sorely missed his drinking pal, heard other bells, like the ones which ring out from wreck buoys on dark nights.

In the village, however, life went on, as it inevitably does. As the mutters of sympathy died, one, by one Granny, Rénard, Buissard - and even Dédé - got involved with the mayor's new Gîtes — and how cunningly that village authority weaved his materialistic little web! To one he offered the job of cutting the lawn, another would be paid to water the flowers, a third would clean floors, a fourth would cook and sew. Soon Lulu's misfortune had become the promise of a little fortune for everyone in the village and in the local bar, on the increasingly frequent occasions when Lulu wasn't around, his neighbours discussed how they would repaint their facades, or buy new car covers, or have a day trip out to La Rochelle when the Gîtes were finished and they started earning all that lovely money - and if Lulu did happen to appear, he was greeted with uneasy silence.

He hung himself on the day that Lourdaud and his gang of masons, started work on the new Gîtes. It was Lourdaud who found him. Stung by a - hitherto unheard of - access of guilty conscience, he'd popped over to Lulu's to complete a long-overdue job of mending a leak in his roof. It was Lourdaud's lunch break and he later told the other builders that seeing Lulu strung up like that – "like a capon strung up by it's scrawny neck," - had quite put him off his chicken baguette.

"He's real unlucky is Lourdaud. First his wife leaves him and now this," commiserated his mates.

The doctor told Lulu how lucky he was. "You're a very lucky man indeed," he said as he tutted disapprovingly and patched up Lulu's weeping neck. A few days later he decreed the Lulu was fit enough to leave hospital and an ambulance, with flashing blue lights, brought him back to his house with all mod-cons, overlooking Mouzon's graveyard.

To everyone's surprise, upon his return Lulu seemed quite sprightly. This 'recovery' suited everyone. It was a thorn out of the communal side. "He's got it out of his system now. He'll soon be as right as rain," everyone said.

He took to visiting the new Gîtes - even complimenting the workmen on their progress - and he took to showing off his weeping neck sores to neighbours, the butcher and even perfect strangers, and you had to look very closely indeed to see his heart wasn't really in it. And a month after his return from hospital, Lulu borrowed a shotgun and blew his brains out.

We were packing the last load into our sturdy 2CV and preparing to leave for a new home and a new life, when we heard the shot. We giggled wickedly, thinking it was probably just another hunter who'd shot off some vital part of his anatomy whilst drunkenly cleaning his gun. Then a door banged open, and then another, and when we heard the echo of Dédé's clogs on the tarmac outside we realised it was a little more serious than that.

He hoved into sight round the bend in the road leading from the cemetery - he was running towards the church. He ran past it and stopped outside the Gîtes. His face was as red as if he'd drunk a whole bottle of *'Gnole'* on his own. He stood there, staring up at the tall building, his mouth working furiously. The workman hung off the scaffolding staring down at him curiously, wondering what was up.

"Il est mort! Il est MORT!" Dédé finally managed to shriek and the tears started bucketing down his pixy-wizened cheeks.

There was a low murmur and one, by one the workers vanished behind their green scaffolding net. Doors creaked ajar, then

161

slammed shut when people heard the news. Our own threshold became a demarcation line, as some instinct warned us to keep our youth and insouciance discreet, in the face of age and tragedy.

Granny appeared, followed by Renard with his flies undone. They stood on the square listening horrorstruck, as Dédé described how he'd discovered Lulu's lifeless body. He'd gone to invite him for a drink at the bar, but he'd knocked and knocked and no-one had answered. There was a sound of running water, so he'd thought Lulu was probably taking a shower. The door was open so he'd stepped inside and found himself standing up to his ankles in blood and gore.

It seemed that Lulu had been worried about messing up his brand new house with all 'mod-cons', so he'd shot himself whilst standing under the shower, thinking that the running water would wash away all trace of his miserable life. Unfortunately his brains had blocked the drains and by the time Dédé arrived, the house was awash with Lulu's gory remains.

An ambulance came. Whooping sirens rang out in the silence of Mouzon's usual Sunday calm. I mused that there was something awesome about violent death in a tiny village - not only because everyone knew everyone else, so the person who'd just done away with himself was probably chatting to you over the hedge about his cabbages just the day before – but because the seismic tremor of suffering which is blotted up by the paper of a million urban lives - and most city dwellers have attained that ultimate level of sophistication of being able to discuss suicide dispassionately over coffee and croissants – becomes magnified like thunder in sparsely populated rural areas and it may take several weeks for villagers to reach the stage of broaching the topic calmly from behind the comforting ramparts of a five-course dinner.

Granny bustled about, covering up the mirrors in Lulu's house, stopping the clock and tracing a cross in chalk on the dead man's door. She'd forgotten we were leaving Mouzon today.

We packed the last of our scanty possessions and headed - metaphorically on tiptoe so as not the disturb the bleak hush - for the car. We didn't drive off straight away, however. Fabrice sat hunched, motionless over the wheel and I shed a few tears. We were sad for Lulu, and we were sad for ourselves – for this terrible omen which had cast it's shadow over our big day. Finally Fabrice turned the key in the car's ignition. The car juddered forward. Pots and pans rattled. The cat peed on the backseat. Renard emerged from the shadows. "You're off then?" he said lifelessly. His face was like an allegorical ivory statue - it looked as if it had been

163

carved to represent 'been-there-before-and-seen-it-once-too-often' weariness.

Fabrice threw up the 2CV's glassy ear flaps and we shook hands all round. Renard's leathery paw trembled an instant in mine and he coughed, as if he was about to say something momentous. "Now do you see where it gets you – all this tourism?" he finally muttered and when we drove away he was staring sightlessly at the village square and his glaucomatous pupils were veiled by a bleary haze of tears.

CHAPTER FOURTEEN

With a flurry it all started to happen. The grant went through at the beginning of October, the bank agreed to a loan and by late Autumn we had workmen scattering fag ash, swearing, staggering under the weight of five-litre wine boxes, slogging back *'Gnole'* or comforting their hangovers with cups of dark, viscous coffee from morning, to noon, from noon, to night, hawking, cussing, bawling, hanging from ladders, upended like bats from beams in the roof, or stomping like china shop bulls all over our new house.

"Don't want this *merde*, do you Madame?" grunted one as I entered the living room after a leisurely stroll in the fag-butt littered garden. Just time for my eyes to adjust to the gloomy light and see the cruel axe glint as it was raised high, and I flung myself bodily in front of the wood-panelled cupboards to stop them from becoming instant matchwood.

Our builders were cowboys and this was our fault, according to villagers. "You bargained over quotes, so now they're taking it out on your house," they said.

It was true, we did haggle, but for the good reason that the quotes we got were utterly ridiculous. Initially we'd approached companies from the surrounding area. Naïvely, we'd thought they would give us a good price, a) Because we were neighbours, b) Because they'd be competing with each other, and c) Because, as a guesthouse, we'd be playing host to foreigners seeking to buy houses and therefore could be seen as a source of future income. To our astonishment, however, *messieurs* Petit, and *messieurs* Boeuf didn't give a hoot about a, b, or c. They came on separate days and petrified us with tales of each other's professional lacunae. Petit said Boeuf had been responsible for most of the blocked cesspits in the area and Boeuf swore blind that more than half of Petit's clients had died, electrocuted. The thing these two entrepreneurs seemed to agree upon, however, was ripping us off. Their estimates arrived within hours of each other and were both incredibly exorbitant. "I get the feeling they take us for imbeciles," Fabrice said dryly.

Since our budget didn't stretch to the pleasure of allowing us to pay builders double what they were worth, we took the risk of putting local noses out of joint and contacted a firm near Angoulême. 'The firm' was fronted by monsieur Benetto, a 'do a deal' Parisian in his mid-fifties, with shifty eyes, a tatty Mercedes and mysterious Italian origins. Benetto was cheap, but still not cheap enough for our meagre budget, so Fabrice set to work on wearing him down. Benetto was resilient and revoltingly sly, but faced with Fabrice's bulldozing techniques - which included pestering him with daily phonecalls, or calling in at his office whenever we were in town to quibble over the price of tiny details on his quote, things like sink washers - the wily Italian gave way and signed a quote which was two-thirds of his original estimate, and far more suited to our scanty resources. In return for his *largesse*, however, Benetto now considered it his God-given right to wander through our home with pockets full of cash, perorating airily on the charms of chrome and Formica whilst offering, with a bored air – "As a favour, you understand?" – to take some *merde*, such as an antique marble fireplace, or an ornate bathtub, off our hands - and when we refused we'd hear his workmen, like a veiled threat in the background, going ape-shit with chainsaws and sledgehammers.

Benetto's workmen were the dodgiest set of individuals I've ever had the dubious pleasure of setting eyes on. There was

Monsieur Rouge-gorge, the roofer, who had a wooden leg which he wedged through the rafters like a peg, for extra security. There was Marcel, the one-eyed plasterer, whose harelip and dreadful stammer combined with alcohol, made him unintelligible after midday. The, there were Bernard and Thierry, two middle-aged electricians who bickered like a pair of spinster aunts and made my blood run cold with their quarrels about which wires were live, and which ones weren't, and who was going to prove he was right to the other one, by stuffing a live wire right where it would do him most good.

Antoine, the tiler, was another petrifying member of this constructor's chamber of horrors. An angular sexagenarian in the last stages of some ghastly wasting disease, he was seized with spasms from time to time and hollered *'Merde!'*, or *"Fils de Pute!"* at the top of his voice. No-one seemed to pay him any mind.. Out in the garden the terracing team was led by a man who had 'I love Mum' tattoos on his fat, fleshy arms. This was Brou, who also had large sweaty palms, a prison past, and a digger of which he was inordinately proud. Brou also fancied himself as a bit of a lady's man and was constantly inviting me to try out his digger, then doing violent things with it at a hairsbreadth from the walls when I refused. Even Fabrice, who was used to the seamier side of

French life, was appalled. "It is like his building materials: Benetto got this lot at knock-down prices," I heard him mutter.

And since Fabrice was off prospecting for work most days - and Benetto was too busy wheeling and dealing bigger projects to give a hoot - the delightful task of surveying this cross-eyed, big-eared, bat-brained bunch fell to me.

On mornings when they arrived grumpy with hangovers, the calm of the house was disturbed only by the regular thump of the concrete mixer, Brou taking the occasional wrong turn with his digger and the jangling accordions of Radio France, Limoges. After a long, liquid lunch in the local café, however, the fun would generally begin. By the first coffee break Bernard and Thierry had usually come to blows several times and been separated by Brou, for whom any excuse to enter the house and boast about his digger, was a boon. Playing tricks on Monsieur Rouge-gorge was another favourite post-prandial divertissement and from time to time we'd hear him holler for someone to come and unstick him from the rafters, because someone else had sneaked up behind him and smeared superglue on his wooden leg. By the second 'coffee' break the idea that there was a woman in the house had got hold of the minds of this bunch of lewd erectors and from my vantage point up a ladder with a paintbrush, I'd be beguiled by the erotic adventures of *'Lili peau-de-chien'* and his 'wagging tail', or 'Jeanneton' who took his 'scythe' to meet three young ladies, and ended up 'harvesting' in various, incongruous positions. This particularly dirty little ditty ended with the edifying moral that if men are 'filthy pigs', it is because women love men who are filthy pigs (and this chorus was roared off-key three, or four times for my benefit). Unfortunately some of the tunes were quite catchy and I would find myself in town of a Saturday morning, battling through the supermarket crowds and absentmindedly humming them, to the scandal of fellow-shoppers who turned in their tracks to stare after this blond bag-lady spattered in pink paint and chanting: "Valentina had the tiniest little nipples and the cutest bottom made of softest silk.."

Unlike his renovating henchmen, Benetto-the-boss was less interested in fleshly pleasures. His overwhelming passion was money. He loved Marks, Yens, Forints and even, it was rumoured, had a yearning for Slovenian Tolars. For Benetto there were no barriers to currency and his conversations were studded with tales of mysterious trips to countries full of eastern promise, where overstuffed cases of unmarked notes changed hands. As for inflation, he worshipped the financial phenomenon – only think of all those extra notes! – and he often boasted how he'd offered a Dinar bath to a Yugoslav lover, greatly impressing her, but costing him, he hastened to add, the price of a few cubic metres of boring water in terms of 'real money'.

In the way others appreciate root-ginger, Benetto's approach to the root-of-all-evil was highly sensual. He loved to caress it with calloused fingers, he loved to press it to his hooter and revel in it's fish-and-chip smell. If someone invented a Cordon Bleu dish brewed out of raw cash, Benetto would have been the first taker. Money was the spice in his dish of life - that element Abba so foolishly described as 'funny in a rich man's world', was serious stuff to him and when he spoke of hard cash his fingers started to twitch, his lips quivered and he stuttered uncontrollably. Which was why, having sidled in to do yet another Antiques Road Show tour of our house one Sunday afternon, we heard him bellowing excitedly from the top floor. When we climbed the creaking stairs we found him on his knees in the dust in front of a massive iron safe. "These miserly Charentais hide all their cash in places like this," he gibbered. "Don't you realize there could be a fortune inside this box?" He rubbed his hands, pulled up the sleeves of his spotless white jacket, loosened his wide black leather tie and shuffled forward on the knees of his Sunday-best wine-coloured flares. "We've got to take a look," he said and he pressed his ear to the safe and starting fiddling with the combination.

After a half-an hour he stood up and gave the safe a loving kick. "I'll go fetch my metal grinder," he said. In the doorway he swung round to face Fabrice. "Seventy- thirty," he bawled.

He'd obviously hoped to catch him off his guard, but he was to be disappointed. "Surely you mean thirty-seventy,? said Fabrice, without turning a hair.

Thirty-seventy ?" Benetto cried aghast. "But it's my grinder!"

"And it's my safe."

"That safe belongs to the people who owned this house."

"I'll give it back to them then."

Benetto's eyes nearly shot out of their sockets. "Surely you wouldn't do anything so foolish?" he whimpered.

Fabrice stared off at the opposite wall. "Try me," he said.

Benetto bowed his head. "Fifty-fifty?" He whimpered.

Fabrice considered an instant. "Sixty-forty," he said.

They shook on it. It was a solemn moment. Then Benetto sidled out to fetch his mean machine.

On that warm Sunday morning in late autumn, the tiny village of Vibrac lay dozing in a sun-drunken stupor. Cats snoozing across half-open doorways dreamt of catching big, fat rats, villagers lounging in wicker chairs dreamt of catching big, fat boars and the air was full of the smell of big, fat geese, basted in garlic sauce and slowly roasting over spits, ready for Sunday lunch.

Benetto returned an hour later, his grinder hidden under a rainmac. He staggered across the floor towards us., still in his Sunday-best, like an ageing John Travolta with excruciating backache. "This might be criminal, so you've got to be subtle - you don't want everyone to know what you're up to," he explained. "I'm taking mother to church after", he added pointing to his wine-coloured flares, then he kneeled to his own God and plates shattered in the house next door, cats yowled and fled and villagers shot out of wicker chairs and fell to the floor with a heavy thud, as he ripped the Sunday calm to shreds with the subtle whine of his grinder.

All afternoon Benetto ground away at the safe, only pausing to order beer and sandwiches from us, with the lordly air of one who knows he is already a millionaire. Finally the door fell to the floor with a thud. Benetto sat back on his heels and rubbed his hands. He was terrifying to see. Metal dust had lined the wrinkles of his face, ageing him out of all recognition. Snags in the floorboard had pulled threads in his wine flares, his white jacket was thick with dust and his leather tie had wrapped itself round the grinder, nearly strangling him, and was shredded, now, to a short, black knot. The only thing still easy to recognise was his avaricious expression. He stuck his head inside the safe and pulled it out again almost instantly. Anguish had replaced avarice in his beady black eyes. "I don't believe it," he muttered.

I bent down and looked inside the safe. There were three large shelves. Two of the shelves were empty and on the third shelf there was a round box with 'Camembert' stamped on the lid. Next to it lay a rag doll, without a head, and a small rusted tin.

Benetto stared into middle-distance an instant, then he winked at me. "I think I've cracked it," he said. "Bloody mean Charentais'd have to do a lot more than that to fool me." And he picked up the Camembert and shook it triumphantly. "This might look like a humble, rotten, lousy piece of Camembert to you, but you can bet you're bottom dollar it's really the place where some nasty old miser's hidden his life savings." He confided and with a magician's flourish he whipped off the lid. A stench of sweaty feet rose into the warm air. Benetto gave a loud shriek and thrust the box away from him, as if it contained a nest of snakes. The box hit the opposite wall and a spongy, mouldered disc bounced out across the floor. "*Nom-de-bleu* it is a bloody Camembert!" he said.

Feverishly now, he fiddled in the safe and pulled out the tin box. He shook it suspiciously. It rattled. He grinned, as if to say 'now we're onto something' and prised off the top. He tipped the box into his sweating palm and a dozen rusted metal buttons rolled out. He stared at them. Turned the box upside down and stared inside it. Then he stared at us. His eyes were hollow, his cheeks were gaunt. "I don't believe it," he whispered. Almost crying with frustration now, he grabbed the doll and ripped open its bodice, then put a hand up it's skirt. "You're not going to tell me that a safe, which has been locked for God-knows how long, only contains a rotted cheese, a tin of buttons and a headless doll?" He whimpered. He shook the doll furiously , then tore off one of its legs and in sheer, absent-minded fury started chewing it. "No-one in the world can be that mean, can they?" I heard him moan.

He left for church in his bedraggled Sunday best, hair stuck out like a golliwog, with the headless doll stuffed in his pocket and a couple of Pineau's inside him to give him courage. He was a broken man.

A couple of days later the phone rang. "Hello is there anyone there?" I said.

Silence. Could this be my first ever obscene Charente phone call? No, it was Madame Fort. "It's about my safe," she finally said.

"You see we left it up in the lumber room - we weren't going to bother with it. But now my son says he wants it to make a mini-bar, so I want it back."

We called Benetto. He was as petrified as if he'd robbed the Bank of France. "Tell her it's been stolen," he hissed. "Then we'll have to get rid of the evidence."

I called Madame Fort and said the safe had been stolen. " Stolen from our lumber room?" She shrieked. "I'm calling the police!"

Hearing the word 'police', Benetto turned up a few hours later. He sneaked in the back way with something hidden under his grubby mac. It was his grinder.. "We 'ave to dispose of the evidence," he said hoarsely and for three hours, solid, he ground away at the safe until there was nothing left, except metal confetti. Then he stuffed the glittering metal, like piece of eight, into a large sack and waited till dark, slurping our Pineau and spying out of the window to check we weren't being watched. Later that evening he finally sidled out with his lumpy bag, looking even more suspicious, if possible, than when he'd first sidled in

Just to play safe I called the police and reported the so-called 'robbery'.

"Silly cow! If she wanted the strongbox she should have taken it with her when she left - according to French law it became yours when you bought the house," they said. But when Benetto phoned me the following evening and told me, in a muffled whisper, that the safe was now part of the foundations of a brand new bungalow near Montemboeuf, I didn't have the heart to tell him it belonged to us anyway.

If Montemboeuf was our nearest 'large' town, it was also the only place within a 20 kilometre radius that boasted a petrol pump and Ferdinand, the owner, knew us well. When times were hard we'd shuffle shame-faced up to the pump and ask for 'five francs worth of petrol, please', like kids in a sweet shop asking for a bag of Sherbet. Born of another age, Ferdinand didn't turn a hair - why, he remembered when it only cost five francs to fill a tank like ours. Ahh, those were the days! Ferdinand's life was punctuated with pump tales. He'd lived next to the gleaming fixture all his life, along with an ageing mother and ageless brother, and he worshipped it like those 'filthy foreigners' worshipped their Buddha.

Diesel came in on Ferdinand's 50th birthday and it was a big shock. Ignoring his howls of protest, the petrol company insisted on installing a second pump, but for many long and miserable months Ferdinand refused to even look at it. The neglected pump grew dowdy and the once lustrous siphon had become a sorry sight, until - egged on by the diktat of extra traffic and the exigencies of an uneasy conscience - Ferdinand finally gave in and started using diesel. These days the interloper was so well accepted that when Fabrice, deep in conversation one day, inadvertently leaned on the gleaming fixture, Ferdinand sulked for a week claiming his careless touch had caused the pump's enamel to peel.

Bright and breezy when the wind was in the right quarter, gruff and grumpy when his Hernia had him by the short hairs, all alone at his post Ferdinand had had time to develop what he called 'his theories'. Dredged up from old school primers, conversations with folks passing through and weird facts gleaned from late-night telly, some of them were extremely odd. He had theories about the world being square, (disease, he said, was caused by people rubbing up against the planet's 'sharp corners) about Gendarmes being little green people from another planet (this explained why nobody like them) and his favourite theory – and one he repeated often for my benefit - had it that Lochness monster was nothing more than a giant otter.

Neither Ferdinand, nor his brother, Jardiland, had ever married. The pair of them had lived in two rooms of faded wallpaper with mother, above the pump, since their pale little legs had protruded from the cradle – and probably would do so, as far as Ferdinand was concerned, until the same pale legs protruded from the mouth of the grave. Recently, however, Jardiland had started acting funny and Ferdinand reckoned it was since he'd retired. With surprising ease Jardiland had slithered out of his old life of mended blue overalls and evenings in with the telly, and slithered into a new one of wearing flowery Hawaiian shirts and taking jaunts out in his electric car, to the seaside. Scratching a late-life itch which seemed to be developing into full-blown Urticaria, Jardiland had also discovered hitherto unsuspected pleasures with the carnal connivance of a 70-years young Montemboeuf widow, who mother had baptised 'Jezebel'.

Well-past retirement age himself, Ferdinand remained faithful to mother and the pumps. Unlike his roving brother, he'd never ever seen the sea. In fact in his whole life he'd never travelled further than La Rochfoucaud. "Out there, they're all savages," he was fond of saying, as he waved a finger in the direction of Angoulême and picked at a pimple on his Scout-shorted, hairy leg, reflectively.

'Out there,' was where we came from. But even if Ferdinand was suspicious of my British accent - and often railed against 'those filthy, fascist countries which still had kings and queens' - his petrol, eked out in spoonfuls, certainly helped us to survive.

Until we had our guesthouse up and running we had no form of income, whatsoever and we discovered, to our surprise, that being poor was amazingly time-consuming. When you're penniless, poverty itself is an ongoing problem that requires constant solutions. Whether it was the wearing refrain of, "how the hell are we going to pay this bill?" or less frequently recurring questions like, "how do I dress for the doctor's when I haven't got a single scrap of underwear?" our brains were permanently stretched on the rack of financial exigency, constantly tortured to come up with a solution - or else!

With money near inexistent, paying for the slightest thing became a matter of tortuous discussion and when it came to using a last five-franc piece, non-paupers would surely be astounded at the surprising variety of choices. These included: buying a stamp to send an urgent begging letter, purchasing the cheapest spaghetti for one last bloated dinner, or spending our last coppers on a candle to light in the church, thus putting our faith in outside forces - and, inevitably, the spaghetti dinner won. As for our car, in the context of such grinding poverty it was the ultimate nightmare.

Having served us faithfully, for so long, our poor old 2CV was on it's last legs. We'd returned from what was laughingly called a 'shopping trip' buying a boot-load of tinned tomatoes, when a motor veered round the corner on the wrong side of the road and hit us head on. "You want us to pay out for that?" sneered the pimply creature sent by the insurance company to investigate. He sneaked a quick look under the bonnet to make sure there was really a motor inside and offered us a measly 200 francs to repair it. The money went on food and the car stayed the way it was.

With one headlamp drooping sadly on a level with the bumper, a caved in bonnet held together with string, a chassis with more holes in it than a colander and a windscreen with more masking tape, than glass, our trusty old banger could have modelled for Picasso's 'Guernica'. The ignition had packed up some time before and in order to get round this minor problem Fabrice, who was not the most patient of DIY guys, had ripped out the dashboard and to start the car he simply grabbed handfuls of brightly coloured wires and rubbed them together until something happened. As we puttered down the road at 5kmph it was not unusual for our badly handicapped banger to coil up and start coughing, like an old geezer addicted to chewing baccy, then spew out a volley of spark plugs. This particularly nasty habit was particularly embarrassing in town, when old dame's would stare after us, thunderstruck, as their darling pet poodles coiled up on the floor, coated with grease and whimpering in pain.

Another embarrassing feature was the exhaust pipe. Fixed to the chassis with binder's twine, it had an unnerving habit of dropping off with an almighty clatter in the middle of crowded streets. Often, as Fabrice grovelled on his belly amongst scoffing shoppers to tie it back on, I would slide, with a stealth born of long practice, beneath the gutted dashboard. Even the discomfort of nestling in a filthy pot-noodle of dangerously sparking wires, was better than the horrendous mortification of being recognised at the wheel of our battered car.

Utterly appalled at the state of our vehicle, a well-meaning relative made the mistake of giving Fabrice a cast-off bag of epoxy resin and various coloured paint sprays. 'Well, it can't look any worse!" he quipped, gaily setting to.

Surveying the Dalmatian nightmare a few hours later - great blobs of resin shoved into gaping, rusted holes, then sprayed with whatever colour had come to hand – I shook my head. "Oh yes it can!" I said.

If the outside of our car seemed like an insult to the very concept of motoring aesthetics, the interior, which supported an entire eco-system, was a boon to the natural world. A sub-tropical climate produced by the heating - which was the only feature in our vehicle that worked *too* well - had combined with water seepage from the leaking, canvas roof to provide the perfect environment for various fungi - which popped up daily in the most unlikely places – and a balmy micro-climate which was ideal for various members of the insect world. Often, as we farted sparkplugs gaily on our way into town, fat white caterpillars would lope nonchalantly into view, spiders, hanging Tarzan-like from fresh-spun threads, would swing unexpectedly into our faces when the car turned a sharp corner and Bluebottles buzzed contentedly, as they raised entire families - incubating them just under heated windscreen, teaching them to fly around the protected car area, rearing them in the backseat - then finally quit the world to die, cremated, in a whizzing, buzzing flurry down one of the heating vents.

Other special features of our tursty vehicle included a faulty clasp on the bonnet, which meant it yawned open at high speeds and had to be held down with an arm stretched, like a tentacle, through one of the flapping side windows. There was something – we never found out what - which kept up an irritating, high-pitched squeal in the front wheels and a particularly unusual feature – and one that was highly popular with neighbours who cadged a lift - was the floor, or lack of it, on the passenger side. Held together by a thin film of rust and a few well-placed prayers, this *Gruyère* of holes allowed the fortunate person seated beside the driver to indulge in the restful pleasure of watching the road slip by directly beneath their feet. When we reached our destination the most sprightly elderly hitchhikers staggered from our car, bodies pleated as if they'd been mauled by some mad Origami hand. This was because they'd spent the entire journey with their feet held high in the air, and their eyes fixed with horror on the yawning chasm. Most of them staggered over to the nearest church and offered up thanks for their safe arrival, or staggered to the bar and drowned their terror in *'Gnole',* but rare were those who ever took up our offer of a round trip.

As for spectacular breakdowns, we collected them and had quite a number to our credit. The accelerator had jammed twice, once – an understandably hair-raising experience – on the Parisian ring road and once on a crowded street – and, of course, when the brake pedal decided to go uncooperatively floppy we were descending a steep hill. But by far the most impressive incident had to be when the starter motor caught fire as we drove onto a busy supermarket parking lot, causing mayhem on a scale which has rarely been seen outside blockbuster epics, like Arthur Haley's 'Airport' - in fact we'd become such veterans at finding slopes to park on when the battery died, stripping tights (mine) in a crowded street to use as a fan belt, or siphoning off petrol without swallowing more than half a litre, there were times we even found ourselves wondering if people with new cars didn't sometimes get bored.

CHAPTER FIFTEEN

It was Fabrice's brilliant idea to enrol me on a cookery course. Since we were opening a guest house, I'd probably have to cook and he'd found that, if I did do a course, the State would pay me for it - all I had to do to be eligible was to prove I'd worked a certain number of hours in the past five years.

We visited the employment exchange (ANPE) to check there was a course on offer, then we headed for the Dole office (ASSEDIC) who would 'yea' or 'nay' my application. A beak-nosed creature guarding this job-seekers bastion was utterly categorical: vile descendants of those scummy Plantagenets who'd bred countless, freckle-skinned bastards to local women during 'The Hundred Years War' could not be allowed to do courses here in France - in other words the years I'd worked in England could not - and would not! - be taken into account. I was in despair. It had seemed such an ideal solution to all our problems and here we were in front of another shut door.

"Remember what I told you?" said Fabrice and he dragged me, moaning, to the ASSEDIC's overseeing body, the *'Direction Départemental du Travail et de l'Emploi'*.

I slumped down in a chair by the door muttering softly to myself. "What a waste of time! If one official says English hours don't count, why should another one, slightly higher up the chain, say: 'yes they do?'" I grumbled.

The woman from the DDTE was young. She had dyed red hair, wore jeans and thought it was a good thing - all these English buying up houses no-one else wanted. As categorical as her beak-nosed counterpart she assured us that the hours I'd worked in England would be taken into account. Then she picked up a telephone and pulled a few strings.

A week later I found myself driving down a muddy lane some five kilometres from Vibrac, towards a draughty village hall where, for nine, long months, I would learn to steam, broil, fry, batter and baste and be paid to do so by the French government - may I just take this opportunity to say, 'thank you very much?'

Weak-chinned, bear-eyed, spotty nosed and - like most of the class - vaguely in his middle 40's, Jean-Marie was the only man in our group of 13 women and on the first day of 'school' there was a hiss of disgust from 12 of them, when they discovered that teacher, too, was female. They'd been conditioned to want a man in authority. They needed a cardboard cut out with initials Mr., to play up to, flirt with, show off in front of and generally keep their female egos warm on those long – metaphorical - nights which they traversed each bitching, classroom-day in the company of a dozen of their own fair sex. The women needed a man and since spotty, weak-chinned Jean-Marie was the only sad apology-for-one to hand, he found himself constantly obliged to do things that, on a beach or in a crowded room, would normally fall to the more muscled members of his kind. When we made pancakes JM had to toss his the highest, so they most of them ended up stuck to the ceiling and teacher had to call in workmen to peel them off, and when we made fishcakes, JM had to root in the bin for a cod skeleton and chase teacher all around the room. He put too much rum in his Babas and they caught light in the oven and nearly burnt the school down, he put gunpowder, scraped out of his hunting bullets, into a soufflé and it exploded and the day we made Chantilly cream he lost control of his electric beater and splattered everyone's clothes. He was the token man in a roomful of women, so he had to louder than anyone else, more vulgar than anyone else, more bragging than anyone else - and even on days when his witty *'repartée'* seemed to have 'reparted' without him, he seemed to feel it was his moral duty to talk back to teacher.

Jean-Marie adored the 'Fab Four' and told me so repeatedly in class. During endless lunch breaks he'd warble their songs at me. "Hey stewed, don't you be fried," he'd croon and be outraged when I could not tell him what the words – his words – really meant. "Are you sure you are really Angleesh?" he'd say, sniffing the air as if he would sniff out this impostor.

In French song mode he loved to do horrible things to Edith Piaf. *"J'ai deux amours, mon pays, et Jean-Marie,"* he'd drone and then pause significantly, waiting for me to understand that he was referring to his hero, that other Jean-Marie known as, 'Le Pen'.

One of JM's more irritating habits was to parrot this champion at every possible opportunity. "The French nationality must be inherited, or merited," he'd say pompously, when I moaned about problems with my *carte de séjour* - and if his team lost a match he'd quote his hero's comments about, 'the difficulties certain members of the French football team have in remembering the words of 'their' National Anthem', adding a far less equivocal: "It's like Le Pen says, French football is riddled with wops and niggers."

JM's ultimate dream was to write a Will, leaving all his earthly possessions to the National Front - if only his wife would let him! "Just imagine - at the *Toussaint* when all the other poor imbeciles have boring relatives standing at their gravesides, I will have *Monsieur* le Pen standing next to mine!" he'd brag - and these visions of posthumous glory were far too powerful to be swayed by a flurry of press articles, telling of others who'd done the same and found themselves buried in nothing more glorious than a cardboard box. Confronted with such evidence JM would sneer and speak of 'journalistic conspiracies'. Well-doped by his favourite party, he was suspicious of everyone (except his hero) and was convinced that the entire world was lurking down sinister back alleys, just waiting to get him.

Surprisingly, when it came to Le Pen some of the women disagreed with their token male. Some of them said he was a fas..fash.. that thing their parents fought against during WWII. Others, whose parents had collaborated, said nothing, whilst one, or two could be heard muttering that, say what you like you had to hand it to Le Pen, he'd got his sums right: after all there *were* three million immigrants, and there *were* three million unemployed.

When I suggested that Hitler had used similar arithmetic to justify the deaths of millions of innocent people, they just sniggered. "Le Pen isn't Hitler. Le Pen is French," they said.

Most of these women had left school at the age of 14, few of them had had more than a couple of years of casual employment in their lives. They got by on the dole and the means-tested RMI and after years of surviving on society's outer fringes, they were just about unemployable. And yet they were virulent when it came to condemning beggars, or gypsies, or anyone who clung to an even lower rung of the social ladder than they did. If they'd have grouped together they could have constituted a force for change. Divided by their own paranoia they were the cannon fodder of men like JM Le Pen.

Sometimes, during these eternal lunch breaks and never-ending coffee hours, I felt like a spelunker trapped in a cave deep in the earth's bowels. In reality I was just a townie lost in the heart of rural France and it was hardly surprising that there were times when I felt a little claustrophobic. When I got too bored to bear it anymore, I played association games, which went like this:

"Arabs?"

"They eat couscous, smell funny and take our jobs".

"Young people?"

"They're lazy and don't want to work".

"Beggars?"

"Too lazy to get a job."

And thus I beguiled away another dull half-hour by pumping the depths of their limited psyches.

One afternoon teacher told us we were going to discuss Parisian food and since I was the only one who'd ever been, I found myself in the odd position of describing the French Capital and it's gastronomic delights, to the French themselves.

Pigalle raised a storm of interest and the Champs Elysées, and it's rich-bitch restaurants, raised a lot of "Ooohs!" and "Aaahs!" But the 'arty-farty' charms of the Latin quarter sank into a muttered-pool of derision, out of which words like 'bourgeois', and 'intellectual' leapt like terrified small fry.

Whilst my fellow classmates paused to digest, Jean-Marie's bony fingers fluttered high. "My Great Aunt lives in Paris - right near the big bridge. Do you know it?" he said and he proudly showed me the photo of a dilapidated hovel, nestling under the iron girder of some anonymous Parisian motorway. When I shook my head he stared at me incredulously. "You don't know my aunt's house in Paris?" he said and I could tell that, as far as he was concerned, I'd lost all my street-cred.

As for teacher, she showed similar incredulity when it came to my cooking skills. As an '*Anglaise*' I was the butt of every joke. Not nasty, necessarily, just utterly inevitable, because everyone knew that the English couldn't cook. Because A + B = C.

There was no point in saying that my mother was Dutch and that I was brought up on a diet of *Kroketten* and *Spekulaas,*. Like it, or not I'd been crowned Queen of my country's so-called lack of culinary skills and just as so many of my compatriots consider that a frog would be naked without it's beret, and 'France' and 'garlic' are synonymous, so my classmates were convinced that I was a useless cook because I was English, and that the only substance I couldn't turn into something fouler, was bottled water.

Teacher was riddled with this culinary *à priori* and even on days when I managed to turn out perfectly edible dishes, she would pull a face and tell the class: "You can tell it's cooked by an *Anglaise*: just by it's nasty flavour.." Such tautological tosh might have bugged me, if I hadn't sneaked into the kitchen that very afternoon and swapped the dish she was turning her nose up at, with another one made by Jean-Marie.

All too often the classroom conversation turned to 'English food' and, inevitably, someone would pipe up with, "You English are disgusting, because you eat salt mixed with sugar."

If I pressed for examples of these so-called barbaric eating habits, I'd hear apocryphal tales of someone, who knew someone else, who was sent to England to learn the language - or die in the attempt - and was shut up in a draughty - generally haunted - manor house, with a batty, bowler-hatted Lord, who fed them ham and jam sandwiches for the duration of their stay. It was no use denying I didn't sneak off from class each night and dine on similar ham/jam delicacies myself, either – they wouldn't have believed me. Instead, I tried riposting with clever sallies, like: 'Well what about Duck in orange sauce - that's sweet and sour and you French eat that?"

Unfortunately this kind of sally was a bit too close to the bone for comfort and generally raised a storm of protest, which ended with someone bellowing, "And you burn your meat, as well!", which has to be the culinary equivalent of: 'I think, therefore I am' - a sort of ultimate 'un-toppable' gastronomic truth when it came to summing up France's case against the English, and their 'disgusting food'.

Most days in class I sat next to a fat-faced French girl, who had a big blob of nose and cheeks like a road map of veins, with minor tracks, made up of broken ones, radiating out from under her chin. She was called Catherine. At lunch one day, wolfing down the starter, then asking for seconds of both the main course and the pudding, Catherine confided that she had high cholesterol. I tried to look suitably surprised. She described her evening meal to me. "We have rich liver pâté, a steak when we can afford it" – she bared her teeth – "all blue and bloody, yum, yum! We usually have chips with it and then some cheese and desert. I usually make *Crème caramel,* but not like the muck teacher makes." Her chins wobbled with laughter. "When I make *Crème caramel* I use nine eggs."

Nine eggs! "And what about your little problem of cholesterol?" I asked.

She shrugged. "I cook for my man and he won't eat less than three courses and then, when I cook it makes me hungry, so..," she shrugged again.

"*On n'y peut rien,*" I thought. For some reason I was reminded of the days when I'd worked as an au-pair for a bourgeois family in the 16th arrondissement. Whilst mum and dad had swanned out to functions and gala dinners every night, their growing kids sat down to dinners composed entirely of packet mashed-potato, plastic ham and chemical desserts. So what did these two tales have in common? Perhaps, the fact that neither type of menu really corresponds with what constitutes most people's idea of 'cordon bleu cuisine'. But old habits die hard - just as the French considered the English to be, without exception, dreadful cooks, it went without saying that they considered themselves to be, without exception, superb chefs. Even if they weren't.

Still pursuing her immutable logic, teacher decided to team me up with the worst cook in the class - this was Agnes. Now, Agnes and I were both in our late twenties and we both had the usual number of arms and legs, but all other resemblance stopped there. Whereas I wore well-cut jeans and loose-fitting shirts to class, Agnes came to school clad in synthetic calf-length skirts, which stretched and shone over her big backside and those sort-of cute, fluffy jumpers which go out of shape after the first wash, and out of fashion soon after. Whereas my hands were fairly well-manicured, Agnes' nails were bitten to a nub and her hands were rough and reddened with patches of untreated eczema. Whereas I wore my hair back from my face in a neat, blond bob, Agnes' mop of greasy hair, held back with an elastic band, had generally escaped by midday and flopped into all her awful afternoon's culinary efforts.

Agnes was on the course because her boyfriend Serge – who figured prominently in all her conversations - had threatened to leave her if she didn't learn to cook. Serge, she confided, was threatening daily to return home to his mother. It must be said, he had a point. Agnes had a positive talent for burning things. She'd forget her boiled eggs and cook them to a cinder, she fried meat until it shrunk to a child-size piece of shoe leather and when Agnes broiled vegetables they generally disappeared in clouds of vapour. To accompany these inedible offerings she doled up a similarly inedible range of plastic sauces, born out of an absent-minded habit of leaving the wrappings on vital ingredients, like butter and cheese. Rumour had it that Agnes had even found a way of burning water, and my ultimate mortification was to see teacher taste my partner's effort, screw up her face in disgust, taste mine and say with a hideously patronising air: "If you keep this up you'll soon be as good as Agnes!"

Every day whilst I pummelled and simmered, sautéed and stewed, Agnes broiled-over beside me, her mane flopping everywhere and her mares eyes wild with fright, as she did incredibly daft things with egg yolks. Side by side over our stoves each day, harnessed like two shire horses to the same culinary cart, we soon became quite friendly. Agnes had never travelled aboard and she listened wide-eyed to my tales of other countries. Then it was my turn to listen wide-eyed as she described her life here in Charente.

One morning she arrived at school all excited. For the first time in the nine-and-a-half years they'd been together, Serge had booked them a summer holiday. "Of course I'll have to start saving now," she confided, brushing back her oily mop of hair and going instantly gray with flour. "Serge says it's up to the woman to pay all the housekeeping and the bills, which doesn't leave me much to put by. I'll have to pay for half the campsite, the petrol and all the visits," she added, scratching her nose thoughtfully and smearing it with snotty, yellow egg yolk. "Of course he does earn more than me - but then he is saving up to pay himself a motorbike," she concluded magnanamously.

The exciting holiday, which Serge had booked already in December and six long months in advance, was to Vassivière, a manmade lake, just outside of the town of Limoges and about an hour-and-a-half's drive away. I tried to imagine getting excited about this – and failed. But if Serge was taking her to the moon, Agnes couldn't have been more thrilled. She chattered about the clothes she'd take, the big funfair she's heard about. She confided that she'd never learnt to swim, but she'd heard she could have lessons. Then she told me more about Serge. They'd been going out together since she was 15, but had only started living together recently because Serge, who'd lived with his parents until the ago of 30, had said he didn't want to lose his independence. She paused to show me a creased photo of her loved one. I found myself staring into a pair of cold, piggy eyes, framed with pale pink eyelashes. Serge was a natural blonde she confided proudly, and she said his job was 'something to do with taxes'.

She slipped the photo back into her pocket then hesitantly confided that Serge had 'one awful fault'. "Serge is horribly stingy", she said.

I was intrigued. What did she mean when she said 'horribly stingy'? I asked.

She gave me an example. It seemed she'd celebrated her 25th birthday recently and Serge had made a big thing about giving her a present. "He went on and on about it. He kept telling me what a great present it was and how it would improve my cooking out of all recognition. I was so excited. Usually he just buys me bath salts or cheap perfume from the local supermarket, so when I unwrapped it I nearly cried. His present was this really expensive

199

food mixer." She sighed and after chewing on a floury nail, pulled it from her mouth with a soft, damp pop and stuck it back in the mess of pastry she was kneading.. "Once I'd unwrapped it he told me how much it cost," she said. "And then he gave me the receipt. He told me my cooking was really lousy and this would improve it. He said I could pay him back in a couple of weeks.."

"I see what you mean," I said.

Another time they'd run out of petrol near a petrol station. Even though Serge had some cash on him, he'd insisted it was Agnes' turn to pay and he'd waited in the warm car, whilst she'd trudged a couple of kilometres, in drizzling rain, to the bank, then back again to pay for the petrol.

After listening to a few more tales like this, I had an overwhelming desire to meet the pig-eyed Serge and reduce him to a quivering pulp. But if I ventured criticism, she would tell me that he was 'better than most'. That he was 'steady' and 'didn't drink'.

As the weeks went by I learnt more and more about Agnes' appalling life. She'd been brought up '*à la dur*'; an awful expression which could hardly be translated by the term 'strict upbringing'. Agnes was one of ten children and beatings from a drunken father, going hungry, or queuing for food parcels had been her daily lot - no wonder the pig-eyed Serge seemed like such a boon! She told me how her father had once beaten a younger brother so badly he'd broken the little boy's leg. "He was only eight years old and he crawled around the house for two days? before dad would pay for the doctor to come," she explained.

Words like 'death' and 'illness' studded her everyday speech and one day she casually dropped a: "Before my brothers died," into the conversation.

"What did they die of?" I asked, horrified.

"Jean-Tou had cirrhosis of the liver and Jean-Louis committed suicide," she said calmly.

"How old were they?"

"Jean Louis was 29 and Jean-Tou had just turned 31," she said.

I'd read statistics saying that France had the highest suicide rate of 25-35 year olds in Europe, but Agnes words turned the meaningless figures into stark - and startling - reality.

Our morbid conversation was interrupted by Catherine's arrival. She was puffing heavily and her lardy face was covered with bright, red welts. This was nothing new. Everyone in the class knew her boyfriend got his kicks out of beating her up.

CHAPTER SIXTEEN

Apart from my cookery course and Fabrice's sporadic job-hunting, our life was one long round of painting and decorating - with occasional breaks to explore the surrounding countryside - now. On our rare days off, we'd follow one of the endless footpaths which led across fields and into the wildest forests and one mizzly morning a shot rang out ahead of us. A few moments later a streak of petrified ginger fled howling past, then a hunter emerged from the bushes. "Have you seen my dog ?" he asked.

I pointed in the direction of the fleeing ginger streak and enquired what was wrong with him.

The hunter turned crimson and stared down at his muddy boots. "I inadvertently shot him in the backside," he muttered.

After that, I took to singing 'Old Macdonald had a farm', and similar silly ditties whenever I was in the woods, just to make sure some drunken hunter didn't mistake me for a wild boar and 'inadvertently' shoot me in the backside.

And somewhere deep in the heart of the forest, Fabrice would generally declare - "This is an excellent place for finding Ceps." - and I'd stare around me, seeking the key - was it something in the air? Did he have some sixth – fungal – sense, I'd wonder?

Then he would point to some guy with a bulging bag, rummaging through thick ferns opposite, and say hoarsely, "Look at that bloke over there - he's got loads of them!"

Fabrice was passionate about fungus, something which, initially, I found very odd. As far as I was concerned, mushrooms were just those maggoty things you found scattered on the top of frozen pizzas – what was there to make a fuss about? - and how come, when every day in other countries the papers were full of torrid tales of murders done for love, or money, in Charente, during the mushroom season, they'd be chock-a-block with horrid accounts of mushroom hunters who'd blown away a neighbour for a fistful of Ceps?

It was only when I started hunting them myself that I understood. There was something so soothing about flitting, alone, under a canopy of oak, beech and chestnut, seeking hidden treasure. It was like being under the sea, only with oxygen.

Everything was bottle-green and the magpies glided above like Manta Rays. And then the coral-coloured 'Girolles' on fluorescent moss beds and the jet-black 'Trumpets of Death' which tooted out from under piles of autumn oak leaves, were nothing like those plasticky, maggoty things you got on frozen pizzas - these mushrooms had flavour. They tasted of nuts and milk and butter and earth. And then, ever since Fabrice had read the mushroom book's chapter about the symptoms of poisoning out-loud to me with ghoulish delectation - "Your limbs start trembling uncontrollably, your pulse starts banging like a steam hammer, your tongue lolls slackly in your mouth, your eyes roll up to show the whites, then your intestines turn liquid and - if you're lucky - you die a few minutes later in the most ghastly, awful agony"- I felt like a bit of a daredevil eating wild mushrooms – like the Japanese must do when they eat those poisoned fish.

On other days we unwound by taking a stroll around isolated hamlets. We'd peer into other people's gardens, admire their magnificent leeks, thieve a cutting or two, or simply steal an idea. We'd amble down potholed roads where chickens scratched in manure, which seeped out from under crumbled barn doorways with the rich smell of rotted fruit. Pigs would roll in the mud in front of us and geese would rush out honking at our passage. We wandered into cool, mediaeval churches and sat in pews smelling of beeswax and mould, to admire the pillars carved with fat, grinning cats and ghouls with their heads between their legs - and increasingly, even in the most out-of-the-way villages, we started noticing more and more houses that were being renovated.

"There's one!" Fabrice would hiss, grabbing my arm and pointing at some middle-aged gent with salt and pepper hair, clad in shorts and a straw hat and weeding a garden that was laid out in careful disarray. From time, to time the weeder would lean on his fork and admire the plot, arbouring the kind of expression others wear when they've just given blood. "There you go nature - I've done my little bit, now it's your turn," his satisfied expression seemed to say.

"I told you so – he is an English," Fabrice would crow triumphantly, and he revelled in this little I-Spy game. It must be said, he knew all the tell-tale signs. Wherever there were clumps of lavender planted next to a neatly tended bed of nettles, or sweet peas trailing over rustic wooden trellises, or rock gardens, or immaculate sloping lawns dotted with cute ceramic pigs; if there was an ageing Labrador, floral curtains, macramé hanging plant holders, or concertinaed paper lamp shades, he declared that there were Brits in residence. As an ultimate test he would fix the weeder over the hedge and wait to see what happened. If the victim met Fabrice's stare with a wave and a hearty 'Bonjour', this would mean Fabrice had got it wrong and the victim was probably French. But if he looked up with a vague smile, flushed bright crimson and glanced hurriedly away, then Fabrice could be 99 % sure he was right and this was, indeed, an *Anglais*.

In town Fabrice played a slightly different version of 'the game'. He was able to identify the adult of the species, here, because of their casual - some would say scruffy - clothing and not-terribly-stylish-but-ever-so-practical-in-hot-climates sort-of hairstyles. In fact as a general rule, he knew that anyone covered in paint, or who looked like they'd just crawled out from under a hedge because they were in the caravan until the house was done, was likely to be English. Other tell-tale signs were socks in sandals, easy maintenance crimplene shorts, pierced noses, badly bleached hair, or just about anyone seen striding down the street bawling, "No, Rover!. Rover I said 'no!'" after a welsh corgi gone berserk, or seen behind the wheel of a Volvo which had a roof rack, or paying too much attention to the ingredients on food wrappings in the local supermarket, or getting jostled in queues and apologizing for it – and any single, one of these tell-tale signs made Fabrice's day, because it meant he could legitimately nudge me in the ribs and crow: "See! I told you so - it's an English!"

One afternoon, out walking near Chasseneuil, however, it was my turn to point out a short, stout woman in her mid-fifties in earnest conversation with an elderly French neighbour. "She's English," I told Fabrice.

He was utterly astounded by my perspicacity. "How can you tell at this distance?" he said.

I decided to let him in on a few trade secrets. "It's because she laughs at everything the other woman says," I explained and I revealed the complexities of this nervous, English, tic to him – how, if we don't speak the language very well, we laugh a lot as if to say, 'I might not be able to communicate with you, but I want you to know that I am nice'.

Fabrice stared at me for long moments, utterly lost for words; here was a concept that he just could not grasp. "But this is France - why on earth would you bother letting anyone know you're nice?" he finally stammered.

Daubed with paint and splashed with glue, crippled with arm-ache, back-ache and aches, where aches had hitherto seemed impossible, we'd finished decorating the huge house, waved a joyous farewell to Benetto and his butcher-band of builders and were left with a bare shell to complete. Our unnerving task, now, was to furnish a Guesthouse, which had six bedrooms and as many bathrooms, two living rooms, a kitchen, a small Gîte and a host of furnishable nooks and crannies, for the princely sum of 50,000 francs.

Luckily, in a murky Angoulême back street we'd discovered a place called the '*Vente aux Enchères*', where, if you were prepared to mix with grim-faced professionals, slack-cheeked dealers and a couple of geezers in grubby rain Macs, you could pick up some astounding bargains.

To my utter amazement no-one seemed interested in 1930's furniture – and I loved it! There were cherry wood buffets with ornate brass handles, there were claw-footed dining tables and wardrobes with carved wood panels - and I soon discovered, since no-one wanted this 'junk', that if I waited until the very limit of the auctioneer's - very limited - patience and then put in a ridiculously low bid, nine times, out of ten, the hammer came down with a bang and I got the goods. Maybe this cost me something in blushes, when the male-dominated room swung round to stare at this single female interloper, but it was well worth it for the host of antiques we got at seriously knock-down prices.

Returning from one of these forays with our old - and now multi-coloured - 2CV groaning under the load of a tallboy-type wardrobe tied to the roof with twine and a nice, oak buffet spewing from the open boot, and with both of us muffled up to the eyes in scarves to ward off noxious exhaust fumes, we were spotted by a couple of policeman on motorbikes. As if our bizarre appearance wasn't enough to arouse their suspicions, at the very instant their heavily goggled eyes stared mournfully into mine, Fabrice was horsing around with a broken leg of the oak buffet. "I know what you're thinking, punk. Did I fire six shots, or only five?" he was growling and bullets were still ricocheting round the car, when the sirens started to wail. Fabrice hastily stowed away the most powerful handgun in the world and set his ruffled clothes to rights. "Oh *putain*! They're sure to fine us, either for overloading, or just for looking plain weird," he groaned.

"Look on the bright side - at least they can't get us for speeding," I quipped.

The cops pulled us over to the side of the road and dismounted on self-consciously bandy legs, ferociously chewing gum. The one on the left banana-peeled the gloves from his pale, white hands with the skill of a Banana Republic *tortionnaire*, whilst his right-hand man stared at us through thick goggles, breathing heavily. Their uniforms were impeccable - the buttons pitilessly reflected the state of our battered vehicle. "You do know that your car is hopelessly overloaded?", said the left-hand cop mournfully.

"Oh, yes, officer – but, officer, I can explain!" gurgled Fabrice and then, like a wave against a rock, his voice broke off in a long echoing sigh. It was too late: left-hand's right-hand man was already writing out a ticket.

Fabrice peered over his shoulder fearfully. "How much?" he asked.

The cop held up five hairy fingers. .

"Five hundred francs," Fabrice choked.

The cop shook his head, chewed on his gum some more, then handed the pen and paper to left-hand and held up four, more hairy fingers.

Fabrice's eyes nearly started out of his head. "N-nine hundred francs? You're fining us nine hundred francs for looking like weirdos? Why that's outrageous - that's just plain, downright, daylight.."

"Daylight, what?" left-hand cop – who was writing the ticket now - enquired, deceptively gentle. He glanced up and I saw Fabrice's strangled features reflected in his Yves-St-Laurent sunglasses.

"Why, plain, downright, daylight *normality*, officer," squeaked Fabrice.

I stared at him disgust, then did the only thing possible, given the circumstances - I burst into tears.

The cop took off his glasses and fixed me uneasily. "*Allons!* You're not telling me you're crying like that for a measly little motoring fine?" he asked.

I nodded pathetically. I was doing my best to remember every lousy thing that had happened to us since coming here - the poverty, the problems getting a grant, the difficulties of being accepted – so I could bawl a little more. It was utterly pathetic and I didn't think it would do the slightest bit of good, but, boy, was I enjoying getting it all off my chest!

Left-hand scratched his head, then he turned to his goggled mate and spread his hands wide. Goggles shrugged at him and scratched his thick, red neck.

Left-hand turned to me again. "You are English?" he asked.

I nodded.

"But I thought you English were stoical and had such stiff upper lips and all that?" he said.

This time when I squeezed out a few more tears, they were ones of silent rage. How many times had I heard that bloody cliché since I'd moved to France? If I got angry on the 'phone, or upset in someone's office, out came that remark about 'stiff upper lips'. But, why did they all want me to have mandibles the texture of cardboard, for heaven's sake? Couldn't they understand that one of the reasons I came to France was to relax my much-maligned labia, for a while? Didn't I have the right, as a fully paid up member of the human race, to experience - and even revel in - my own emotions just like the French did?

I wanted to tell these two men in uniform that it was my parents generation who went out in the midday sun and had fun with mad dogs – not me! I wanted to explain that only British men in their middle fifties couldn't cry - even if they had the most reasons to - and that no-one had told ever told me wanking would make me deaf. I wanted to say so many things, but how could they understand? We were two nations separated by the same channel tunnel and would never see eye-to-eye. So, instead, I just spluttered, "And I hate Benny Hill!" and left it at that.

The pair of them stared at me for a long, lingering moment of vague surprise, then goggles was called away to his bike radio and the *tortionnaire* just sort of wandered off down the grassy bank.

As I watched, he got down on his hands and knees and started rooting about in the earth. "What on earth is he doing?" I said, fascinated despite myself.

"Probably looking for snails," Fabrice said gloomily.

I considered this. "But it hasn't rained. He can't be looking for snails," I said.

Goggles came back minus his defining feature. "You're lucky. We've been called out on an urgent job, and we don't have time.." - was that a wink? - "..to write you a ticket," he said. He tore the paper up and it blew out over our car like wedding confetti. It was a wink!

Oh thank you officer," I bleated, revoltingly abject.

The *tortionnaire* had climbed back up the grassy bank, now, and was standing behind goggles with one hand behind his back. I went weak at the knees. Perhaps he had a gun. Perhaps he was going to murder us for making so much fuss over a stupid motoring fine and perhaps that's what he'd been looking for down that grassy bank - somewhere to dispose of our bodies!

He stooped to the window and his shadow blotted out all my sun. I wanted to plead with him to be gentle with me, but my throat had gone unaccountably dry. There was a nail-biting screech as his revolver scraped up against our piebald paintwork. I

213

shut my eyes and prayed. When I opened them again he was holding out a bunch of violets. "For you," he said solemnly.

I was still gawping in amazement, five minutes later, when he mounted his powerful steed with a cowboy flourish, nodded to his goggled partner and the two of them rode slowly off into the magnificent, pink sunset.

CHAPTER SEVENTEEN

We'd finally done it! Everything 'everyone' had said we'd never, ever manage on such a tight budget - buying a house, renovating it and purchasing all the fixtures and fittings - we'd done it and in the early Spring of 1990, we opened for business.

Already, a few months on, signs put up along the busy main road at Chasseneuil had brought holiday traffic in the shape of a busy Swiss family, several, boisterous Germans and a carload of fun-loving Spaniards. To our vague surprise, however, of local folk's families down for the Easter holidays, we hadn't yet seen a dickey bird.

We were all the more mystified, because we'd done everything we could to avoid being labelled a 'tourist ghetto'. We'd had people in for drinks, put up posters in the supermarket inviting locals to come in and have a look around - we'd even offered special cut rates for the family's of local residents. It seemed like the right thing to do. Since most of our neighbours had sisters who came down on long visits from Paris, or brothers up for Easter, or maiden aunts prone to drop in for an unexpected spate of grave-hopping, we thought there was an enormous potential market for our guesthouse locally and yet - even though our rooms were larger, our toilets were a lot cleaner, we had no tricky chairs with three legs, or beds with hollow mattresses - neighbours kept on acting as if we didn't exist and sending their relations to the - far more expensive - local hotel. It wasn't until our posters were hanging limp in the supermarket that we found out why this was.

Fabrice was in town for the day and I was making beds when a woman in her late fifties, with hair fresh out of curlers and clad in a blue, flowered housecoat knocked on the door. "I'd like a room," she said and her voice went suddenly deep. "For the afternoon," she added.

My first thought was that she must be unwell. "Perhaps you would you like an aspirin?" I enquired.

She gave me the tight-cheeked stare of a camel about to spit. "I ask for a room and she offers me an aspirin – as if I'd be here if I had a headache," she muttered.

"Then, perhaps you'd just like to lie down for a moment?" I suggested, bewildered.

She snorted. "I only live five minutes down the road, so if I wanted to lie down I wouldn't have far to go, would I?" She darted a quick look over her shoulder and shuffled closer "You see I do want to lie down, but I want to do it in the biblical sense, *heh, heh,*" she added and she nudged me a few times to make sure the message hit home.

I stared at her in horror. "If you live next door, why don't you do it in your own house?" I asked.

"Because of the Mother-in-Law," she snarled. "Since my hubby died, in mysterious circumstances at the fun-fair a couple of years back, the miserable old bag won't let me bring another man into the house."

"I'm sorry, but I can't do that - this is isn't a brothel, you know," I spluttered.

She winked slyly. "You don't have to pretend with me. We saw all those workers going in and out every day, when your husband was away," she said and with a lewd snigger, she left.

We laughed about it, of course. After all, we'd expected some rumours - that we were smuggling drugs, for example; we'd heard it said so many times about young people who moved into the area, before - "After all, how else can they survive?" said local logic.

And we were only mildly surprised when Granny, who had it from the baker, who'd had it from the grocer, told me that, seeing us driving back and forth with car-loads of furniture each week, our new neighbours had decided we must be bare-faced burglars, who did our jobs – like others went to work - as regular as clockwork every Thursday (auction day).

However much I laughed about it with Fabrice, however, out shopping, or in a queue at the village post office on my own I secretly started to dread the moment when someone would whisper, "that's her!", and a sea of curious faces would swivel round to stare at me. I could almost hear the cogs of their memories grinding furiously as they tried to remember what they'd overheard said about me by the butcher's or the baker or his sidekick, the candlestick maker. I tried to dispel this unpleasant 'myth effect', by introducing myself in, what I hoped was, a friendly fashion, but it made not the slightest ounce of difference. After shaking my proffered hand, there would be an interminable silence whilst they sized me up and down and then someone would say, "So you're the one whose bought the old wool house down by the stream, are you?" and there would be silence again, except for a few, significant glances which said they were dying for me to leave the shop, so they could huddle together and discuss me furiously.

It was highly unnerving to be judged, not for what I was, but for what others said I was. It was bizarre, to say the least, to stare into eyes which didn't see me, because they were seeing 'that other one', the fruit of their fearful imagination. I soon discovered this phenomenon was quite implacable. Whether I smiled, or snarled, it didn't make the blindest bit of difference. Because, what I did personally didn't make the blindest bit of difference. Because they didn't see me personally at all - it was their ears that did all the work. When they looked at me, they were remembering all the gossip they'd heard in the street and come hail, or sunshine, smile, or frown I was just a blank canvas on which they painted that 'shameless hussy' who was the rumoured me.

But if personal rumours were unpleasant, it was the slander relating to our business which really hurt the most. Before I'd served up my first meal, the neighbourhood was rife with tales of 'awful English muck'; before anyone had been to stay, tittle-tattle had decreed that our beds were 'hard as iron' and our showers as 'cold as ice'. Having invested our tiny 'all' in this enterprise, believing in it utterly and desperately needing it's source of income, it was heartbreaking to be dismissed out-of-hand, before we'd even had a chance to prove our worth.

At first, Fabrice, who'd got a part-time job, now and spent a lot of his time in town, accused me of rampant paranoia. "Not everyone's yakking about us you know. It's just a few loud mouths near where we live," he said.

And I certainly wanted to believe him. It seemed too awful to consider that people had really started turning to stare at me - even in shops in distant Chasseneuil, and Montemboeuf - just because of stupid gossip. So I ignored my own instinct and all those turning heads, and told myself he was right and I was plain barking paranoid. Until the day when even our old neighbours in Mouzon - people who'd known all of Fabrice's family and seen him as a babe in arms - started giving us what I'd privately baptised, 'The Look', and on that fateful day even Fabrice had to admit I had a point.

I'd describe 'The Look' as a cross between avid curiosity at the scene of an accident, and the reaction to that exciting announcement, 'he's not got long to live." It somehow expressed the notion that the 'Looker' had taken it on trust that the 'one being looked at', was the same as himself, up till now and had suddenly received disturbing - and vaguely titillating - proof of the contrary. When Buissard gave us 'The Look' and Dédé started looking me up and down like one of his sex-shop dolls, it began to dawn on us that in such a tight-knit community where word-of-mouth was more powerful than the internet, what we would have liked to ignore as 'just silly nattering', could have very serious consequences for us – and for our business - indeed.

There were times that I was astounded by the hostility I encountered from people I'd never even met. Old women would turn their heads away when I said 'hello', groups of men would whisper as I passed by and gangs of adolescents would point me out in the street and giggle loudly. "But you don't even know me - why don't you talk with me and judge for yourselves if these rumours are true?" I wanted to say and - far worse than the mortification of being pointed out and laughed at - was the sense of how unfair it all was.

When I whinged about it one day to Renard, however, he just snorted. "You're not the only ones, you know. All the 'new kids' are crucified by gossip here - especially people who set up their own business.," he told me and with apparent relish he related a few, lurid tales of Parisians who'd somehow rubbed someone up the wrong way and found themselves jostled on crowded streets, or refused service in village shops, or whose cats had been hung, drawn and quartered, 'as a lesson'.

His tales made my hair stand on end. If they were true the French countryside sounded more like something out of 'The Godfather', than 'The Good Life'. I comforted myself with the thought that he was probably exaggerating.

"I told you. I've been here 20 years and they still call me the Parisian," he concluded and the way he said it seemed to make it all, somehow, quite legitimate.

To me it was all utterly incomprehensible. Given the odds against living here - the lack of employment, the isolation, the lack of leisure facilities - it seemed to me that local people should be overjoyed if anyone made the effort of trying to settle, here. As for setting up a business, given the odds against ever getting past the red tape, the taxes, the low profit margins, long hours and high overheads, it seemed to me that anyone setting up a business in rural France should be given a gold medal.

"*On n'y peut rien,*" was all that Renard said, when I pressed him. "Everyone goes through it. That's just the way it is," he said.

Granny was kinder and did her best to perk my spirits up. "You just stick it out for five, or six years and you'll see that people will end up accepting you," she said encouragingly.

"Five, or six years?" I said in horror. I knew she meant well, but how could I tell her I'd only had a three-month dose of this treatment and already I woke up at nights screaming?

Maurice told us not to take it seriously either. Maurice was an ironmonger from Paris who'd moved to Charente in the 70's, when 'everyone' was doing it, and after ill-starred adventures, like running a chicken farm and making and selling goats cheese had swallowed up his small capital – and his wife had run off with another man - he' d got by doing what he called 'bits and bobs and odd jobs.' This meant he was always in and out of other people's houses and with his vast number of acquaintances, he always had a few, good stories to tell. Round for coffee he was relating the tale of an elderly farmer who'd 'lost' his tractor.

"Th'old fool had been ploughing his field and sucking on a bottle of *Gnole* at the same time and then he got out off the tractor to piss. What a joke! He couldn't even find his dick, so it wasn't surprising he lost his tractor!" Maurice slurped reflectively on his coffee and scratched his thick gray beard. "Th'old idiot came to see me burbling something about 'tractor thieves'. 'Tractor thieves, my arse!' I told him. We went out to find the field where he was ploughing, but the idiot was so rat-arsed he couldn't even remember which one it was, so we spent all afternoon looking and finally found his tractor right down the bottom of one of the fields, in a ditch. The silly tit was so drunk he didn't notice he'd left the handbrake off and when his back was turned the tractor had just rolled away."

Over a second cup of coffee Maurice got onto the tale of an '*Anglaise*' who'd just bought a house near his. The previous day she'd invited him in for a cup of tea.

His half-crazed eyes glazed with horror at the recollection. "It was hot and I was thirsty so I went in, and I wanted to walk out again it was so totally, bloody, horribly primitive!" He spluttered.

I was intrigued. To hear Maurice, who lived in a cat-infested hovel with an asbestos roof and no electricity or running water, refer to someone else's house as 'primitive' meant it really must have been bad. I asked for more details.

He scratched his beard nervously as if the task was too big to know where to start. "There was no glass in the windows, just plastic sheets," he said slowly. "She has just a floor of beaten mud and she sleeps in middle, with a man called 'Boyfriend', on a mattress, like pigs, wallowing in all that mud. And when I was there it had rained and the room was flooded and the *Anglaise* was wading round, up to her ankles in all that filthy mud." He paused to repeat 'mud' a few times as if soil was the ultimate horror.

I pressed for more details.

He scratched his beard fretfully. "Inside the house - in the room with all that mud - she hatches out chickens in her wood burning stove," he gulped. "Her neck is black like the pipe of a wood burning stove itself, it is thick with filth and she says she sleeps in the same jumper she wears all day – and her man is even worse! He has a head as smooth as the eggs that come from my chicken's bottoms, and he wears a skirt and all the time I was there he kept laughing and telling me he had nothing on underneath and all the while he kept laughing about this!" Maurice's voice rose hysterically. "And when I tried to speak with him, he told me he was reincarnated and originally lived on Mars, and then the *Anglaise* interrupted him and said this was just his little joke, that in reality he came from Venus! And then she insisted on showing me her garden and she had legs sticking out of the pond at the bottom.."

"What do you mean legs?" I asked, startled. So far I'd taken these proofs of my compatriots eccentricity pretty mildly, but now I had a vivid image of some bow-legged Myra Hindley look-a-like sloughing back and forth through a sea of mud and pondering on bodies she'd dismembered, whilst behind her in a crackling stove, cute, yellow chicks popped from their eggs and roasted instantly in a foul odour of singed feathers and the boyfriend cackled madly..

"She told me they were made out of plaster," Maurice croaked breathlessly.

"Ahh, why didn't you say so before? That means that she's an artist and she probably comes from London - *Londres,"* I explained to him.

He nodded, thoughtfully, as though I'd revealed some fundamental truth. "But that wasn't the worst bit. The worst bit was the cup of tea," he continued and his beady eyes disappeared behind a bush of furrowed brow. "You see her neighbour keeps goats in the barn next door, only the goats are never cleaned out and inside the *Anglaise* house is just one, seething, mass of flies," he said and he buzzed fiercely until he saw I'd got the picture. "These flies were everywhere – they kept landing on my hands and taking off from my cheeks, or getting stuck in my beard and when she handed me the cup of tea, three flies fell into it, but she kept watching me so I had to drink it all the same. But do you know what was the worst thing of all?"

I shuddered - what could be possibly worse? Offering him biscuits smeared with manure, perhaps, or a sandwich stuffed with mosquitoes eyeballs? "No I don't know," I said.

He gulped and looked like he was about to be sick. "The *worst* thing of all was that she had put milk in the tea," he confided.

CHAPTER EIGHTEEN

It was like a towering inferno - new rumours were grafted on to old ones and every day the gossip grew louder. Caught up in the eye of this tattling hurricane, watching the walls rise higher and higher around us, I felt strangely helpless, as if I was in the power of forces beyond my control. I found myself trembling uncontrollably outside a shop, or scared to pick up the phone, or answer the door in case I encountered more of that inexplicable hostility. I was slipping down that well-greased chute leading to petrified paranoia and the coalhole of insidious, irrational guilt.

It wasn't helped by friends, either. They advised me to 'just ignore it" and pretty soon, along with the tea and sympathy, I detected a hint of contempt. "Fancy getting so worked up over a couple of silly rumours," I could see them thinking - and I knew it was what they were thinking, because it's what I would have been thinking myself. So I gave up talking about it. I stopped mentioning the half-a-dozen snubs I received each day, I gave up talking about new rumours and perfidious gossip, because I was terrified of the moment when I'd see them sniff the air, as if they were trying to smell the smoke which, in the heart of their logical minds, they were convinced was never there without fire. Not that they really thought that I was a prostitute, or Fabrice was a paedophile - of course not! - it was just that they had great faith in the laws of cause and effect and for them it was obvious: if we were being persecuted like this, it was because we must have done 'something' to deserve it. So they started evolving theories to explain - what they didn't understand - away. One woman told me it was all because I hadn't invited 'so and so' for Sunday lunch, another suggested it was something to do with the way I dressed and a third stated categorically that it was because Fabrice was a Parisian. Just as statisticians manipulate their figures to demonstrate whatever they've set out to prove, our 'friends' started scrutinising aspects of our character, now - little eccentricities which they'd hitherto considered charming, like singing in the rain, or laughing at bad jokes, or being polite to shop assistants - and found them, in the light of current events, eminently suspect.

229

You have to be in the victim's place to understand that all those old sayings are hopelessly wrong. – that sticks and stones can harm you, but so can words. They can cause other wounds, which can't be set in plaster and fester for long years after. How could I fail to feel guilty? Everything was telling me we'd done something wrong - the problem was I had no idea what. So I found myself wishing we really were the villains/prostitutes/bandits we were made out to be. At least then we'd have the compensation of having a boot-load of filthy lucre. Instead of which I had the beginnings of an ulcer and couldn't afford to see a doctor.

Luckily, there was a positive aspect to unceasing conflict - in a woman's sense it was 'making a man of me'. If I could have just run away and hidden myself in the heart of an anonymous town, here, in a tiny close-knit community, I couldn't bury my head in the sand. I had to come to terms with what was happening - and fast!

We had blindly plunged and now we were resurfacing to a whole new set of realities. There were days when the 'againsts' seemed enormous - and on these days we talked wearily of jacking it all in and heading back for town. But each morning when we were woken by a thick mesh of birdsong and the sound of our very own Cockerel tearing the morning calm to shreds with his victorious cock-a-doodle-doo, we remembered why we'd moved here and it was the 'fors' that had the upper hand. So we grinned and bore it. Kept our heads down and slogged on. We put up more signs up, spoke to everyone in sight, put ads in local papers and editions overseas and soon we had a slow, but steady trickle of guests, who came to enjoy their holidays in the old wool house by the stream.

And the months went by and gradually we lifted our heads and look around us and realised the gossip had started to recede - that one, or two villagers had even sent their relations to sleep in our 'iron hard beds'. Our nearest neighbour took to exchanging a few - albeit begrudging - remarks about weather over the garden fence, others nodded in the street, instead of staring and even the butcher, if he didn't exactly smile at us, seemed to frown a few wrinkles less.

Then the summer season started and I spent my days frying onions, braising garlic, basting herbs and toasting spices to make pâtés and fresh salads and creamy platters of *'Porc Soubise'* and steaming casseroles of *'Poulet Marengo'*, just like I'd learnt to do 'at school'. When Fabrice came home from work at night, he helped me, making beds and serving at the table, and for a whole month we were inundated with satisfied guests.

Cautiously we congratulated each other. We even bought a 'new' car, a battered Renault 5. Life seemed to be looking up at last – and then we found the pipe

Of course, we'd seen it before - how could we miss it? It's mouth was the size of a large gargoyle's and it spewed out just opposite our dining-room window. We'd enquired about this pipe before buying the house and - via his sullen-faced secretary - the mayor had assured us it was just an outlet for rainwater. We hadn't wanted to make a fuss - we were hooked on the old wool house by the stream - so we'd told each other we'd disguise the offending conduit with hanging baskets and plenty of ivy and then we'd forgotten all about it. Until now.

With summer temperatures soaring and hardly any water left in the stream, guests had started asking us if we had anything else on the menu, except rotten eggs. Soon it was mid-August. The days were broiling hot and sultry with thunder and the smell got steadily worse. Guests started avoiding the dining room - even at breakfast - and asking for rooms facing away from the charming little river. Reluctantly we were forced to admit we had a problem – that there was something more than rainwater coming out of that big, fat pipe.

With a growing sense of urgency we started making phonecalls, only to find the authorities we called were strangely evasive. Although I described the cloying odour to the *'Eaux and Forêts'* representative, he maintained it was rainwater oozing from that funnel. When I described the thick, brown gunge seeping from our conduit, the man at *'La Chambre d'Agriculture'* said that perhaps – perhaps! – someone was using the cylinder to empty water from their dishwasher - and steadily the smell got worse and the calls got more frantic. Soon we were spending hours on the phone each day pleading with each of the relevant authorities to just come out and take a look, but they wouldn't. "The mayor is 'the police' of his commune," they told us. "If you want us to do something about your problem you have to see the mayor first."

After months of living in gossip's shadow, we were understandably reluctant to do this. Now the tittle-tattle had died down, the last thing we wanted to do was draw attention to ourselves. Not that we knew the mayor - our dealings with him, so far, had always been via his disobliging secretary - but we knew he was a farmer and had a reputation of being *'entière'*, a term which was generally applied to non-castrated bulls and meant one, of two things: either he was a bulldozer when it came to getting things done, or, like a bull, he just charged at anything which got in his way. We hoped it was the former.

On the hard bench outside his office we began to suspect it was probably the latter. *Monsieur le mairie* was discussing footpaths with the representative of a local walking club. "I don't see why the our commune should pay good money because a bunch of namby-pamby prats, who've got nothing better to with their time than go out on poncey walks, are frightened of a few brambles. You can tell your members that if they want the footpaths cleared, to come and see me and I'll lend them a couple of sharp scythes!" we heard him bellow.

When the harassed walkers rep scuttled out a few moments later, we entered the mayor's office like sheep to the slaughter. Summoning up all the feminine charm I could muster I fired him my most winning smile.

He scratched at his clean, white collar irritably. "What d'you want?" he grunted, as if I was just another one of his ornery heifers.

Monsieur le maire reminded me of a bull dressed up in Sunday-best. He looked as out of place in this office surrounded by papers, as we would pitching manure in his farmyard. We were off of different planets and were on a collision course, it was obvious, just from the way he was eyeing Fabrice's stylish rain Mac and pale, pink shirt

Ostentatiously he didn't offer us a seat, so I hopped from one foot to the other as I perorated about our pipe. All the while his close-set eyes - which had difficulty fending a gap between puffy red cheeks - ranged over me ceaselessly. It was highly unnerving to be scrutinized like this. It was as if I was, indeed, a heifer and I was being assessed before being sent to sell at market. When I finished my speech I half-expected him to clip a ticket in my ear and send me off with a hearty whack on the rump. Instead there was a long, uncanny silence and I had time to notice a thick, blue vein - which I hadn't remembered seeing when we entered the room - throbbing alarmingly on his wide, red forehead.

When he finally spoke, the reason for his long silence became clear - he was having difficulty controlling his anger. "That pipe was put there before you were born and no-one's ever complained before," he growled thickly.

"But the house has been empty for more than 25 years, so there was no-one around to complain," I protested.

"And perhaps it would have been better if it had stayed empty," he muttered darkly.

"When we moved here, we asked your secretary about that pipe. She said that you'd said there was only rainwater coming out of it," I said

"There is only rainwater coming out of that pipe," he answered, in a tone that was dangerously even.

I was so exasperated I wanted to scream. Why on earth didn't he believe me? Who, in the world, would want to make up a problem about a stinking pipe? "Why don't you just come and see for yourself?" I pleaded.

"I don't have to come and see. I know it's rainwater," the mayor growled. His puffy cheeks were bright purple, now, and he was so furious he couldn't even look at me.

"But it smells!" I cried.

"If you don't like country smells, you should have bought the house," he snapped.

"But it's not a country smell - and anyway, I didn't know it smelt before I bought the house!" I shrieked. My voice was taking on a distinctly hysterical edge. Fabrice put a hand on my shaking arm to calm me. I took a deep breath and decided to change tack. "We don't want to make a fuss. We wouldn't bother about that pipe if it wasn't such a problem for our guests," I said. "Surely you can understand that it's a problem for us? I mean, how would you like it if you took your family on holiday and your vacation was ruined because your room stunk?"

"My family on holiday?" he roared. "I've never had a holiday in all my life!"

"Well what about other people in the village then - surely you're concerned about them? What about the fishermen, who fish in the stream, what about the kids who play in the water - surely it matters to them if the water is polluted?"

At the word 'polluted' his eyes narrowed, until they were just slits in his bloated cheeks "So you're one of those bloody ecologists, are you?" he roared and he banged on his desk so hard it made me jump. "It's your bloody lot who stop me shooting the buzzards who thieve my corn. It's your bloody lot who won't let me spray pig-shit on my fields!" he ranted. He was breathing heavily now, like a bull about to charge

Seeing my appalled expression, Fabrice tried to draw his fire. "To get back to the problem of that pipe," he said.

The mayor swung to face him like a punch-drink dinosaur. "You bloody, poncey Parisians – you come out here and want to change everything. If your so bothered by our country smells, why don't you go back to bloody Paris where you bloody belong?" he snarled.

Fabrice didn't blench "I might be a 'townie', but even I can tell the difference between the good, old country smell of pig-shit in the fields and the stench of the shit that's coming out of that pipe," he said suavely.

Monsieur le maire rode back in his chair - Fabrice had scored a point. "So you expect me to dig up the whole river just to please you?" He said nastily.

"I'm not asking you to dig up anything., I'm just asking if you might find out why there's raw sewage coming out of that pipe – or, at the very least, carry the pipe further up stream so I don't have to smell it over breakfast," Fabrice said evenly.

"Oh, that's all is it? And whilst we're at it, perhaps we could dig you a swimming pool and turn your garden into St Tropez and let the commune pay for that too?" he said.

Fabrice stayed heroically calm. "All I would like the commune to do is help us solve our problem with this pipe," he said.

But the mayor wasn't even listening. "So you think you have the right to come in here and tell the mayor of his commune what he's supposed to do?" he growled.

"I don't want to tell anyone what to do," Fabrice said, a shade irritably. "I was told that the mayor was the right person to help me solve my problem, so I've come to see the mayor, for help."

"Hotiy-toity problems with pipes - you're troublemakers, that's what you are."

"We have a problem that might put us out of business and because we try and do something about it, you call us trouble makers?" Fabrice said in amazement.

"I've heard about you two – I've heard how you go over people's heads to get what you want."

Fabrice stared at him, as if he couldn't quite believe what he was hearing. "If you're talking about the grant, we didn't go over people's heads," he began.

I interrupted him. "We had no choice - we had to go to the President in Poitiers, otherwise we'd never have got the grant. What else were we supposed to do - just give up?"

"We don't do things like that out here," came the dour reply.

"And perhaps that's why nothing ever gets done," Fabrice said furiously. "If you won't help us, we'll just have to find someone who will!"

The mayor went bright crimson and fiddled with the papers on his desk. 'We'll see," he said.

I was startled by the menace in his voice. "'We'll see' what?" I asked.

"We'll see what happens when you put people's backs up," he snarled. The masks were off now. War had been declared.

"But we haven't put people's backs up - we're just trying to solve a problem that will put us out of business. What else are we supposed to do - just let all our hard work go down the drain?" I cried.

The mayor's silence was eloquent. He stood heavily to his feet. His big nose trembled and his cheeks were the colour of wine stains. "I don't give a monkey's toss what you bloody troublemakers do and I don't give a monkey's toss what happens to your business, but one thing you are going to do - and right now - is get out the hell out of my office!" he growled and without more ado, he shoved us outside.

The door slammed shut behind us and there was the sound of a key turning in the lock.

I stood a moment trying to get my breath back. I hardly knew whether to laugh, or cry. Fabrice gave a feeble smile - his cheeks looked as wan, as mine felt. "Well at least we know where we stand now," he said, in a weak attempt at flippancy.

I gave a mirthless chuckle. "We know where we stand, alright - on the other side of a locked door!" I said bitterly.

CHAPTER NINETEEN

"Department of Health & Sanitation, *oui?*"

"I'd like to speak to someone in charge."

"In charge of what?"

"Pollution problems."

"What for?"

"A problem of pollution."

"Have you spoken to the mayor of your commune about it?"

"Yes. The mayor says he doesn't want to know."

"And what did he say?"

"He said he doesn't want to know."

"I'm afraid you must contact the mayor of your commune and discuss the problem with him. Once you have done this the mayor will get in contact with us."

I stared at the receiver. Could this be a pre-recorded message? "I'm sorry, I don't think you've understood. Someone is polluting the river which runs through my garden and I have seen the mayor and he tells me he won't do a thing about it."

"Well if the mayor won't do a thing, then neither can we," came the tart reply and then the line went dead.

Gritting my teeth, I rang back and got someone else. As briefly as possible I explained about the river and the mayor.

"Well, what do you want me to do about it?" came the disgruntled reply.

"Perhaps you could put me through to someone who can help me?" I suggested.

"If the mayor doesn't want to help you, there's nothing we can do," came the terse response and - 'bang' - the phone went down again.

When I rang back for a third time, I was a whole lot sneakier. I stubbornly refused to give a reason for my call and made vague references to life and death matters - and it worked! A few moments later I was connected with an - albeit minor - official. My triumph was short-lived, however. "So you're the one who's been pestering my secretaries?" he said.

For the sake of progress I decided to crave his bureaucratic indulgence. "It's true, I have called your service a few times, but it wasn't just for the pleasure of annoying your staff, it is because I have a problem which is very likely to put me out of business.," I fawned. Taking his grunt for a sign of interest, I related my tale once more, in terms that would have opened the tear ducts of an average stone. "So you see, I have invested everything in your beautiful country and if I don't find a solution to this problem then I do not know what I shall do," I wound up wildly, leaving acres of tragic possibility - ranging from self-mutilation, to full-blown suicide – dangling in the ether between us.

"I still don't see why you had to be rude to my secretary," he just grunted.

I was stung to the quick. "I wasn't rude to your secretary - if anything she was rude to me," I began. Just in time I caught myself. This man wasn't an administrator for nothing, he had such technique! He'd nearly trapped me into making that fatal mistake, when dealing with French bureaucracy, of saying what I really thought. So when I piped up again my voice was creeping treacle. "I sincerely apologise for any misunderstanding which might have arisen between myself and your secretary. May we not put this little contretemps behind us, now and discuss my problem?" I grovelled.

" 'A misunderstanding' isn't how she puts it. She says you were downright rude," came his phlegmatic response.

This time - I admit it - I lost my rag. "I don't care what she says, what about what I've said? I mean, doesn't it strike you as rather odd that someone should run up massive phone bills just for the pleasure of pestering your secretaries? I mean - and I want your honest opinion now - do you see any, possible logic in such behaviour, especially as - and I'm sure even you can understand this - all I really want to do is find a solution to a problem, which is going to put me out of business?" I screeched.

"Oh well if you going to start being rude to me as well!' he said huffily. This time, however, before he got the chance, it was me who slammed the phone down.

I was forced to admit it – I was going about this in all the wrong way. I was like an amateur ornithologist out to trap a bald eagle with a butterfly net. I was an average *'citoyenne'*, who should've realised by now that in order to corner a civil servant - in order to entice it down from its cosy perch in the branches of that diseased old oak tree which is French bureaucracy – she would have to employ a lot more stealth and cunning. - stay down wind, set traps, slaughter a – metaphorical - goat, or two.

During the long, sleepless nights that followed, I hatched the wildest plans. I imagined doing a long, slow streak, dragging chains and a symbolic length of stinking pipe, past the offices of the water board. I abandoned this project, however, when it occurred to me that, far from drawing attention to our dilemma, such behaviour was likely to be perceived as perfectly normal for an *'Anglaise'*. So I dreamt up another wheeze, which involved slipping into the office of some important *monsieur 'So and So'* and leaving my phone number - along with my (exaggerated) bust measurements and an invitation to 'call me' etched above in red lipstick – in a prominent place on his desk, but this scheme was abandoned too. I reflected that, if the note would surely grab his attention, the anticlimax when he called me and discovered I only wanted to discuss a stinking length of pipe (which wasn't even his), was likely to have the opposite effect to the one desired - and if there was one thing we didn't need right now, it was more enemies.

Finally I just let Fabrice do the calling – a male voice has so much more authority, *n'est-ce pas?* – and after scolding one secretary and dropping a few names to another, Fabrice succeeded where I'd so miserably failed and was put through to the Big Boss himself

'BB' ranked so high in the administrative chain he could even allow himself the luxury of emitting a personal judgment: "It is the same all over France. The mayors have far too much power," he opined. He promised he would call the mayor and 'see what he could do'.

We were cautiously jubilant - could it mean the end was in sight, at last?

Of course it couldn't. 'BB' called the mayor the following day and then he called us back. "The mayor doesn't want to know," he said.

"But we know that already," whined Fabrice.

"Without the mayor's go ahead, I am afraid I am powerless," BB said.

We were back to square one. A couple of minutes later the phone rang and I rushed to pick it up. It was the mayor. "How dare you make a fool of me by going over my head and talking to my superiors. You're going to pay for this!" he screamed.

We weren't even back to square one, anymore, we were a lot further back - and up to our necks in '*la merde*'.

In increasing desperation, we phoned the *Direction Départementale de l'Agriculture* and made a rendezvous with an important official. When we explained that the mayor didn't want to know about our problem, he sniffed suspiciously. "Do you have proof that the pipe is polluting the stream?" he asked.

"It depends what you mean by 'proof'. We have plenty of guests who've seen what's oozing out of that pipe," we replied.

He sneered at this. "That's mere hearsay. If you wish to prove there really is a problem of pollution - and if you hope to get something done about it – I'm afraid you will have to call in a bailiff as your legal witness."

We called a bailiff. He was surprisingly amiable. Warning bells started to jangle deep inside my wallet. "By the way, I suppose you charge?" I said.

He told us his fee was 1,500 francs. We talked it over. 1,500 francs was a whopping amount for us, but it would be worth it, wouldn't it, if it meant our problem was solved?

Just to make sure, Fabrice called the important official at the *Direction Départementale de l'Agriculture* again. "Once I've got the bailiff's statement, will you come in and sort out our problem?" he asked.

The official was astounded at our naivety. "But of course not! This affair has nothing to do with us. Once you have the signed document you must take three copies along to your local gendarmerie and there you must lodge a complaint."

"Lodge a complaint against who?" asked a bewildered Fabrice.

"Why, against the polluter, of course. But in this case, since you have no idea who is causing the pollution, strictly speaking you should lodge a complaint against the entire village."

"You are saying we must go to the local gendarmerie and lodge a complaint against every single member of the village we live in?" Fabrice asked incredulously.

"No, of course not - that would be just silly," the official said.

Fabrice snickered with nervous relief. "Yes it would be silly, wouldn't it? He agreed.

"In order to simplify matters, since the mayor is the village's legal representative, you must lodge a complaint against him," the official went smoothly on.

Fabrice's snicker nearly choked him. "You are telling me I must go to the local gendarmerie and lodge a complaint against the mayor of the village I live in?" He said hoarsely. He could hardly keep the horror out of his voice.

"If you want something done about your problem, yes. Of course, it is my moral duty to warn you the mayor has been mandated to represent the French government and by lodging a complaint against him, you will be pitting yourself – symbolically, at least - against the French government as a whole." He marked a brief pause. "Need I advise you to hire a very good lawyer?" he said.

Fabrice slumped down in his chair next to the phone, like a broken reed. "Are you telling me we have to hire a lawyer as well?" He said weakly.

"It would be highly advisable," the official said cheerily. "Of course it will be very expensive and since it takes years for these sort of cases to go the court, even if you do win it will be quite a while before you get your money back."

A whimper escaped Fabrice's lips. "Are you saying there other cases like ours?" he moaned.

"Oh, hundreds," came the breezy response.

"And yet there's no simpler way to get things done?"

"Of course there's a simpler way".

Fabrice clung to the receiver like a drowning man. "Tell me what it is then – *please!*" he moaned.

"The simpler way would be for the mayor to contact us. If the mayor contacted us your problem could be sorted out in a couple of weeks.," came the implacable response.

"But the mayor doesn't want to know!" shrieked Fabrice.

"I know that," the official said.

"So there's no simpler way?"

"I'm afraid not."

It took several, stiff drinks and a very long walk in the balmy evening air to bring a pinch of philosophy to it all: "None of this will matter in a hundred years from now," we told each other as the first star switched on high above us, like a galactic street lamp. But however much we tried to play it down, the knowledge that we were stuck - that there wasn't a single, blind thing we could do - was still a very bitter pill to swallow Around us the mist swung as softly as a hammock, lulling cows and crickets to sleep. The peaceful night air was perfumed with sour milk and honeysuckle - and the heady aroma of raw sewage. "I'll have a dig in the river tomorrow and see if it' does any good," said Fabrice.

Returning through the darkened village streets, we noticed an official-looking poster pinned to the village notice board. We drew closer and saw our names written large across the top of it. Underneath it we read: "..have complained of odours issuing from the communal rainwater pipe."

I felt vaguely uneasy. "I wonder why they've done that?" I said.

"Dunno. Must be an administrative thing," Fabrice said gloomily.

But it wasn't an 'administrative thing' at all, it was a signal. It said that the phoney war was over and the real hostilities were about to commence.

CHAPTER TWENTY

Up until now our next door neighbour had been careful to keep her hysterical mongrel out of sight. Now, however, she left him out of doors day and night and the tatty loo-brush would fix us with close-set eyes, from behind the garden hedge and yip for hours on end, like some dirty old mutt barking his rocks off. Magnified by the river which separated our two properties, at night the creature's howling cries were like something out of 'The Hound of the Baskervilles' and my winks of uneasy sleep were filled with slavering beasts chasing me across endless plains of quicksand. After a dozen nights of this dog-and-water torture I could take it no more. I decided to tackle the neighbour.

"No-one else has complained about it," she said, as she looked straight through me to a distant point on the horizon.

As usual, no seemed able to advise us about it, either.

"Yip! Yip! Yip! Yap! Yap! Yap!" For a gust of wind, a fluff ball, a passing duck, or a stray ant, for hours on end the mental mongrel kept up it's infernal racket. We were losing guests by the truckload. Even people who'd driven off the motorway for a bit of peace and quiet, checked back into the hotel right alongside it, saying that the four-lane highway was quieter.

Days pass in a daze. Soon I was covered in bruises from walking into chairs, doors – and the occasional lamppost - and Fabrice had multiple burns from nodding off over bubbling saucepans, and waking up just in time to whisk them off the cooker before they bubbled dry and burst into flames.

"Yip! Yip! Yip! Yap! Yap! Yap!"

"Get double glazing put in," suggested the woman who ran the local chemist's. This seemed like an excellent idea - until we got a quote.

"Why not change your whole house around and sleep in the rooms facing away from the river," suggested the girl at the supermarket checkout. Since this would have meant changing the shape of the roof, sleeping in the toilet and putting guests up in the mud-floored cellar, we were loathe to take such drastic steps. Instead we experimented with different brands of ear plugs, but gave that up too, when Fabrice rammed one so far into his ear it took three doctors and a lot of evil-looking scalpels, to remove it.

"Yip! Yip! Yip! Yap! Yap! Yap!"

We hung on, we hung fire. We prayed that the neighbour would break out in a rash of guilty conscience - or her pooch break out in a rash of Bubonic plague. But every day the loo brush with close-set eyes was there at his post, behind the garden hedge and every night he kept up his hysterical yipping and the torture of sleeplessness continued.

Finally, in sheer desperation we called the gendarmerie. "The mayor lays down the law in his own village. If you want to find a solution to your problem, you must call the mayor," they said.

Oh no, not that again!

"Yip! Yip! Yip! Yap! Yap! Yap!"

Reluctantly we called the mayor. "Poncey bloody troublemakers coming out here and trying to change everything. No-one else has complained!" he bawled.

Help from that quarter seemed highly unlikely.

"Yip! Yip! Yip! Yap! Yap! Yap!"

We chatted to an old dame from the village. She sniggered at our naivety and suggested rat poison. Tempting thought it was, this solution seemed a bit drastic. Instead, we made an appointment to see our local '*conseiller*' from the '*Conseil Générale*'.

To our surprise he looked nearly as exhausted as we did. His cheeks hung down in slack folds like a bloodhounds and there were deep pouches beneath his eyes. We told him about the dog, and explained the problem this represented for our guesthouse. "I'm afraid you'll just have to put up with it. You see no-one else complains about this sort of thing," he said tersely.

And we only understood his terseness when we emerged from the house and a pack of hunting dogs, kept in a tiny pen in the house opposite, set up a bloodcurdling howl. Unfortunately, we couldn't 'just put up with it'. Unlike our long-suffering '*conseiller*', we had a business to run. So we picked up the phone again and after hours of calling around, discovered we were entitled to a free consultation with a lawyer at the '*Maison des Avocats*', in Angoulême.

To our astonishment the lady lawyer who received us, seemed exhausted, too. "The only thing to do is send a no-nonsense letter, recorded delivery and with acknowledgement of receipt," she told us wearily and she dictated a formally worded letter to be sent to the dog's owner.

"Surely there has to be some better way of sorting these kind of problems out – surely it should be possible for people to just talk to each other?" I said, when she'd finished.

She snorted. " If you knew how many of these sort of letters I dictate, each and every day," she said.

Damned if you do, damned if you don't: The letter was sent recorded delivery and the cur stopped yipping. Bliss! Unfortunately, if no one had been able to tell us how we *should* have resolved our problem, now that we had done people were unanimous in telling us that the last thing we should have done was what we *did*.

After a leisurely breakfast in the dining room one Sunday morning, we pulled back the curtains to discover a dozen fishermen camped out on our newly planted lawn. One had spread his maggots out on the garden table, another was hauling in a tricky catch over my just-created rockery and a third sat square on an empty terra-cotta plant pot, reading a newspaper - and the pile of pink paper beside him told us this was his 'black hole' of fortune.

Fabrice had the greatest difficulty getting them to budge. "We've always fished here in the past and no-one else has ever complained," they said and when Fabrice suggested that this was probably because the house had been empty for 25 years, they sloped off - grumbling about 'townie troublemakers' who 'thought they owned the place' - leaving behind them a detritus of beer bottles, fag packets and fish hooks which it took us the rest of the morning to clear up.

A few days later we returned from Angoulême to discover hoof prints had torn our, already battered, lawn to ribbons. At the top of the garden the fence had been snipped apart with wire cutters and at the bottom-end the gate stood open wide. When we finally caught up with the horsemen who were responsible, they told us the mayor said our garden was on a right of way. When we showed them cadastral plans to prove this wasn't so, they sneered nastily. "We always used it as a passage before you lived here and no-one else ever complained," they said.

We could no longer kid ourselves that what was happening to us was just a spate of isolated incidents. As unpleasant and petty as it seemed, we were forced to admit we were being deliberately persecuted.

Oddly enough, rather than outrage our dominant emotion was one of guilt. Let's face it: to be hated in this day and age – unless you're filthy rich – is to have 'failed' – and this feeling of shame was the biggest 'danger' we'd met so far. Take this kind of situation too personally - pay too much attention to your reflection in the mirror and before you know it you're on the other side and playing *boules* with the Cheshire cat. Difficult as it was, we had to come to terms with the fact that this unpleasant persecution had little, or nothing to do with us personally - how could it, when we'd never even seen, or spoken to most of our persecutors? – but a great deal to do with what we represented in a tiny village in the heart of the French countryside: in other words, a terrifying force for change.

"You have to understand - you come here to get away from it all, but most of the people who live here would love to get away from all this," he said, and he flung his arm out towards the rolling valley surrounding us.

We were lunching with our notary and a group of his friends, who'd gathered to witness the emptying of the notary's overstocked lake. The sun was astoundingly warm and we sheltered beneath a centennial chestnut tree, eating the notary's mother's homemade liver pâté and listening to the notary's friend, a catholic priest clad in jeans and a black t-shirt and sipping wine, who was telling us about this area where he'd lived and worked for the past 25 years.

"Not that any of them would want to leave *La Charente* of course – far from it," he continued thoughtfully. "I doubt if they could imagine living anywhere else. But it's the space - the sheer emptiness of their lives – they'd like to escape and it's easy to understand. You see, before the TV put in an appearance in the early 70's, they spent time together. In winter there were *bourrées*, where they got together and danced and had fun, and when the weather grew warmer they'd sit out on the steps chatting to each other. There's no doubt their lives were harder half-a-century ago, but at least they shared their troubles, whereas now.." he sighed. "The good old TV's changed all that forever. These days everyone stays inside watching the box and they've forgotten what it is to live together."

All three of us stared solemnly at the empty lake where a pile of silver trout lay floundering, belly up. Suddenly the priest let out a booming laugh. "Did you know that a huge percentage of the older people still vote communist out here?" he said.

I thought of Dédé and his pilgrimage to see Lenin, and nodded.

"It doesn't make matters easier for me, because it means there's a strong, anti-clerical tradition," he said. "It took me a long time to get people's confidence and even now it isn't easy. You see you can get on fine here, if you're like everyone else – and if you don't make waves, people will generally treat you kindly. But if you scare them in anyway - and anyone who wants to change things inevitably will – then I'd say – and I meant it with the full weight of my holy office - God help you!"

Understanding it was one thing, living with persecution was quite another. If each petty incident could easily be dismissed in itself, in the number and duration they started to wear us down. Normally good friends, Fabrice and I took to bickering about the pettiest matters and – inevitably - in the heat of the battle we blamed each other for what was happening. We saw the danger of this just in time, too. That old expression, 'divide and rule' didn't arise out of nowhere. We realised that if we turned *their* anger and *their* frustration in on each other, then all would be lost. The only way either of us could get through this incomprehensible ordeal was to stick together. So that's what we did.

We went on greeting the sporadic guests that autumn brought, we cooked and made beds, smiled and nodded at those of the villagers who still smiled and nodded at us - and tried not to notice all the others who stared as if we had three heads - and when the spate of official visits began, we did our best to grin and bear it.

A sharp rap on the door at 7 am was four men from the fire brigade. "We want to see your fire escapes immediately!" bawled their chief. Once the men-in-blue had swarmed all over our house and assured themselves that we had all the necessary fire-fighting equipment for saving guests in peril, they relaxed enough to accept a cup of coffee. "What made you come and see our place?" I asked the chief curiously.

"We were told your guesthouse didn't respect the 'norms,'" he said, slurping his coffee thirstily.

I handed him a digestive biscuit. He munched on it appreciatively. "And who told you this?" I asked.

He shook his head. "Dunno - it was an anonymous phone call," he said.

The Health and Hygiene officer was summoned by an anonymous phonecall, too. He'd come to inspect our so-called 'sub-standard' kitchen and he skulked through the room, peeking into waste bins and running a disdainful finger over pots and pans, as if we had a body hidden, at least. Unable to find anything out of the ordinary, he quibbled over ceiling heights. "Your ceiling is ¾ of a centimetre lower than the 'norm'," he told us.

Fabrice protested that we'd already had an inspector from Health and Hygiene visit our premises and he'd already given us the green light.

"I'm telling you this ceiling is against the rules and if I want to, I can order you rip it out and redo the entire kitchen," the officer insisted hotly.

"But I know for a fact there are at least half a dozen restaurants round here with a lower ceiling than ours – and what's more their kitchens are filthy!" Fabrice countered with equal heat

The official drew himself up to his full, diminutive, height. "Are you suggesting my department doesn't do it's job, Monsieur?" he enquired nastily.

"No, I'm just saying it wouldn't be normal to make us rip out a brand new kitchen because of a quibble over ¾ of a centimetre," Fabrice said stoically.

"My dear *monsieur,*" the official said haughtily. "The word 'normal' - as you will soon discover - is exactly what I say it is!"

A few days later, when the Fraud squad arrived and gave us an hour's hassle, for a 5 franc slice of camembert which had been charged twice on a customer's bill, we realised that someone, somewhere really had it in for us.. And a couple of days later, when Fabrice returned from work, he found me in tears.

There was a small road just outside our front door and for the third day running, all day long, a gang of local adolescents had ripped up and down the road on whining mopeds. They yelled and swore so loudly, I could hear them wherever I was in the house and whenever I'd emerged to do some gardening I'd been greeted with wet farts and wolf whistles. On the third day I'd had enough and asked them to go and ride their mopeds elsewhere. My words were greeted with jeers and whistles and the noise just got worse. When I finally broke down in tears, it wasn't because of the kids or their mopeds, it was because I felt so utterly helpless. I knew the neighbours wouldn't help me, and the mayor didn't give a hoot - and I certainly didn't want to call the police, who'd tell me to call the mayor. For the first time in my life I was a prisoner in my own home.

"Why didn't you tell me about this?" Fabrice asked, as he mopped up my tears. How could I tell him that, with his chewed-to-a-nub nails and dark-ringed eyes, he was in such a state of nerves himself I hadn't wanted to bother him with one more petty problem?

He phoned the kid's parents. They were strangely uncooperative. "No-one else had complained," they said.

So the kids stayed swearing and shrieking and farting and revving from dawn to dusk, on the road outside our house. With Christmas holidays in the offing and nothing better to do, the crowds began to swell. Groups of adolescents started arriving from other villages and soon there were 30, or 40 of them congregating outside our house every day just for the pleasure, it seemed, of making my life an utter misery. I felt like some harassed celebrity who'd deceived her fans: my every appearance was greeted with catcalls and wolf whistles. When it reached the stage that, even when we were out around town, the mere sound of a moped had me quivering like a blithering jelly, Fabrice decreed we had to do something. The trouble was, neither of us had the slightest idea what.

"They say there're going to make you leave," Granny told us that weekend, when we went to stay at Mouzon to get away from kids on mopeds. I was still pacing up and down the big old draughty kitchen at 3 am. I remembered arriving in this big-bellied old house in the middle of the night – how strange it had all seemed. I remembered how I'd been terrified by the lack of light and the silence. I thought how kindly the neighbours at Mouzon had treated us. I realised what a hard battle it had been to survive here and how much I loved it all now. And I realised I didn't want to leave and no-one was going to make me. "So what are we going to do ?" I asked Fabrice for the hundredth time.

For the hundredth time he shook his head.

"*On n'y peut rien?* Are we going to give up all we've worked so hard to get, just because of some stupid, local mafia?" I nagged.

He shook his head. "There's one thing we can do – and we should have done it from the start." He sighed heavily.. "We can go to the police station and lodge a complaint against the mayor," he said.

I took a deep breath. I'd wanted a drastic solution, but this was too drastic for words. "You realise it could make our life utter hell?" I said.

He laughed bitterly. "What have we got to lose? Our life is utter hell already!" he said.

We drove to the gendarmerie the next morning. We'd talked it all through and decided for maximum sympathy value it would be better if I did the 'helpless female' bit and saw the police on my own. Entering that gendarmerie at the beginning of the new year,

1991, was one of the hardest things I've ever done in my life. The officer in charge informed me, without preamble, that his wife's sister was married to a 'bloke' from the village and he'd already heard all about us. He took down my statement in stony silence. "So you say everyone in the village hates you," he said, when he'd finished.

"Not everyone. Just a few people who are jealous and want to stir up trouble," I said, struggling to remain calm.

He asked me other questions and every one of them was loaded, so that after a gruelling half hour I hardly knew if I was the victim, or the criminal anymore

"And because of a bit of noise you want us to stop the local kids from playing on the public highway?" he concluded.

"I don't want to stop them from playing. I want to stop them from deliberately persecuting me," I replied.

He read the statement over to me and I signed it, then he called another officer and issued some terse commands, then he showed me to the door.

We drove slowly back to Vibrac, talking all the way. When we got to the crown of the hill we parked up near the pine tree, just as we did on the very first day we came to visit, and looked down on the pretty village. We could see our house from afar and the lane we made, the day we decided to cross the Loire. Because we hadn't just crossed a river, we'd crossed over into a whole new way of life.

Heidi Fuller-love was born in Kent, to a Dutch mother and an English father. After running a successful comedy cabaret venue near Lewisham - and guiding misguided Americans on tours of haunted London in her spare time - she moved to France in 1988 and opened a Chambres d'Hôtes. Since then she has written and photographed features for hundreds of French interest magazines, both at home and abroad, and has regular columns in 'French magazine', 'Living France', 'Spanish Homes magazine', 'Design & Architecture' and many others. Her 'Notes from a Spanish Pueblo', a humorous account of buying and renovating a ruin in a tiny pueblo blanco lost in the heart of Andalusia, is a regular slot in 'Everything Spain' magazine.

Heidi Fuller-love now divides her time between a charming hovel in Charente and a half-renovated ruin in Andalusia. Her next book, to be published shortly, is 'A Deadly Mix', the spine-chilling and highly evocative true story of the woman who inspired Flaubert to write Madame Bovary.

ISBN 141202425-0